Selecting a Translation
of the Bible

Selecting a Translation of the Bible

by Lewis Foster

STANDARD PUBLISHING
Cincinnati, Ohio

39975

The following abbreviations are used for these Bible versions:

KJV: *King James Version* or Authorized Version of 1611.
NASB: The *New American Standard Bible,* © The Lockman Foundation 1960, 1962, 1963, 1968, 1971, 1972, 1973, 1975, 1977.
NEB: The *New English Bible,* © The delegates of the Oxford University Press and The Syndics of the Cambridge University Press 1961, 1970. Reprinted by permission.
RSV: *Revised Standard Version* of the Bible, copyrighted 1946, 1952, © 1971, 1973.
GNB: *Good News Bible* or Today's English Version, © American Bible Society, 1966, 1971, 1976.
TLB: *The Living Bible,* copyright 1971 by Tyndale House Publishers, Wheaton, Ill. Used by permission.
NIV: The Holy Bible: *New International Version,* Copyright © 1978 by the New York International Bible Society. Used by permission of Zondervan Bible Publishers.
JB: The *Jerusalem Bible,* copyright © 1966 by Darton, Longman & Todd, Ltd. and Doubleday & Company, Inc. Used by permission of the publisher.
NKJV: The *New King James Version,* © 1982 by Thomas Nelson Publishers. Used by permission.

Photos of ancient Bible versions courtesy of American Bible Society.

Sharing the thoughts of his own heart, the author may express views that are not entirely consistent with those of the publisher.

Library of Congress Cataloging in Publication Data

Foster, Lewis
   Selecting a translation of the Bible.

     1. Bible—Translating.
     2. Bible. English—Versions.
  I. Title.
  BS455.F66 1983   220.5'2   83-4689
  ISBN 0-87239-645-2

CONTENTS

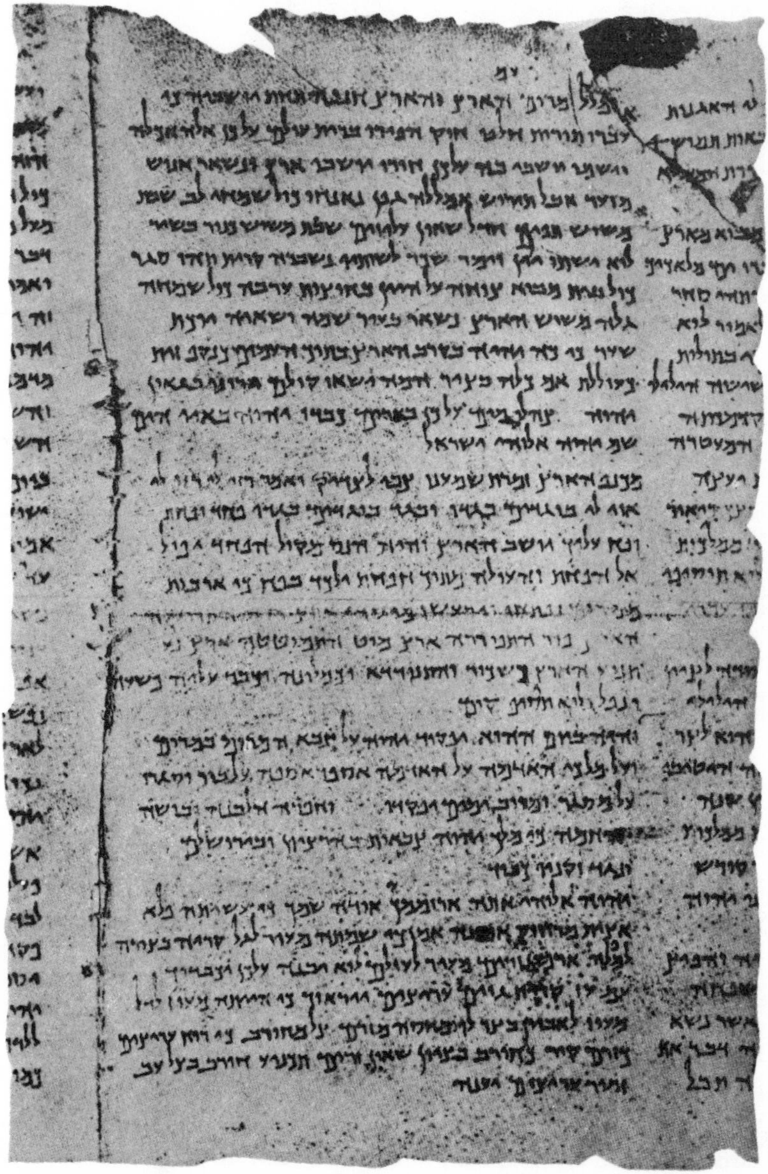

Hebrew text, the Dead Sea Scrolls

Chapter One

FACING THE PROBLEM

ix hundred years ago English-speaking people had a problem. No translation of the whole Bible had been made into English. Only those who could use Hebrew or Greek or one of the languages that already had translations, such as Latin, could read the Word of God for themselves.

Three hundred fifty years ago the problem was different. In the century preceding 1611, at least a dozen different translations of the Bible had been made into English.[1] Now the English-speaking people had gone from no English Bible to so many translations that people were confused and divided. Then King James of England commissioned the outstanding work that became the reigning translation among the Protestants for centuries to come.

About one hundred fifty years ago Alexander Campbell pointed up another problem: The Bible was written in the living language of the people to whom God had originally directed this inspired Word. Did it not stand to reason that, when it was translated into another language, it should be translated in the living language of that people also? But a particular way of expressing oneself remains "living" in a language only as long as the expression reflects current usage. So, Alexander Campbell maintained, at least every two hundred years the Bible should be translated again to keep it in the living language of the people.[2]

Many have come to support the idea of more translations and frequent revisions. In the last fifty years new translations have numbered more than fifty,[3] bringing the total to over five hundred English translations of the Bible or parts of the Bible.[4] Today, one is plagued by problems similar to those of 350 years ago. This flood of translations has brought confusion and question to the minds of many. Are all these translations good? Are all these translations bad? Are some of them better than others? How is one to decide which translation is best for him? The more one knows about translating the Bible, the problems involved, the results in the past, and the attempts in the present, the better one will be able to make the judgment—"Which translation of the Bible?"

WHY MAKE A TRANSLATION?
To make God's Word understandable

The primary necessity for a Bible translation is to help readers understand God's Word. When the people of Judah returned from the Babylonian captivity, they used Scripture in the effort to restore their nation. On a particular day they gathered in Jerusalem in front of the Water Gate for the reading of the Law. As Ezra stood before the people to read, he was flanked on either side by men who "caused the people to understand the law." "So they read in the book in the law of God distinctly, and gave the sense, and caused them to understand the reading" (Nehemiah 8:8). These Jewish people no longer understood the form of Hebrew used to write the Old Testament books. If they were to understand the sense, it had to be explained in Aramaic, for this was the language rapidly spreading throughout Mesopotamia and the eastern Mediterranean for international trade.

One hundred fifty years later (about 280 B.C.) a translation was made into the Greek. This is called the Septuagint (LXX) translation, because 72 Jewish scholars are supposed to have worked on it. The Septuagint was done because Ptolemy Philadelphus wanted to make the Jewish Scriptures understandable to the Greek-speaking people.

Soon after the New Testament was completed, it was translated into Latin. Parts of the Old Testament were translated into Syriac by the first century, and the New Testament was translated into Latin and Syriac by A.D. 150. By A.D. 200 a translation into Coptic had been made in Egypt. In the following centuries versions were made in the Armenian, Gothic, Ethiopic, Georgian, Arabic, and Persian languages.[5]

When men were inspired to write the Scriptures, they wrote in the languages common to the time and place in which they were writing. The Old Testament is written in Hebrew except for passages in Daniel 2:4b—7:28 and Ezra 4:8—6:18. Here the Aramaic is preserved. The New Testament is written entirely in Greek. Some maintain that there was an Aramaic original of Matthew. If this is so, the Aramaic copies have long since perished, and only the Greek remains. But the message of the Scripture is destined for every time and place, and must be translated into the different languages in order to make the truth understandable to all.

To keep God's Word living and accurate

It is necessary to continue making new translations and revising old ones if people are to read the Word of God in their contemporary languages. With the passage of time, words change in meanings. For instance, in King James' day the word *prevent* could mean "come before" but not necessarily in a hindering way. So the translators in that day rendered 1 Thessalonians 4:15, "For this we say unto you by the word of the Lord, that we which are alive and remain unto the coming of the Lord shall not prevent them which are asleep." But today the word *prevent* has lost that earlier meaning ("come before"), so it must be translated differently to convey the proper meaning: "According to the Lord's own word, we tell you that we who are still alive, who are left till the coming of the Lord, will certainly not *precede* those who have fallen asleep" (NIV).

10

If some words change in meaning as time passes, other words drop out of usage altogether. We no longer say, "wist ye not" (Luke 2:49), when we mean, "Did you not know." To keep the translation of God's Word living it must be kept in the living language the people are using.

The primary goal of a translator is to make his translation accurate; that is, to convey faithfully from one language to another the meaning intended by the original author. This accuracy is dependent not only upon the proper choice of words in the translation, but also the preservation of the very words the author used in writing his original work. This is called the study of the text. We conclude what the original text was by comparing the numerous manuscripts that date back through the Middle Ages to the earliest of the written copies from the third century. Today many more of these manuscripts have come to light than were known in the days of King James. Because of this additional knowledge about the text, judgment about some passages has changed. For example, John 1:18, "No man hath seen God at any time; the only begotten Son, which is in the bosom of the Father, he hath declared him" (KJV), has more recently been rendered, "No one has ever seen God, but God the only Son, who is at the Father's side, has made him known" (NIV). In the latter translation Jesus is explicitly called God, the only Son. The judgment of textual scholars has changed at this point because of manuscripts more recently discovered.[6]

As we gain new understanding of the meaning of a passage, discover new manuscripts, and observe new meanings to words, we see an increased necessity for keeping translations of the Bible in focus for succeeding generations.

But what is the other side of the coin? Is it possible to have too many translations of the Bible? Can something be said in favor of having just one translation?

No doubt there is a point at which the continued addition of translations adds confusion rather than contribution to the understanding of God's Word. Some felt that point had been reached in the seventeenth century when the *King James Version* was made. Many have come to that conclusion today. At whatever point we cry, "Too many!" we nevertheless must recognize that translation is a continuing task and that we cannot be locked into one translation forever. On the other hand, no translation should be published without undergoing judgment on the caliber of its work and the fulfillment of explicit purposes for which it was made. Some translations may claim new understanding. But if this understanding is based upon denial of Biblical accounts of miracles or a diluting of the person or teaching of Christ, such starting points are likely to lead away from the proper meaning of a passage. If a translator claims his work to be readable, but is so loose in his translation that he gives his own ideas rather than the significance of the text, he ceases to function as a good translator.

Furthermore, when a preacher reads from one translation and the congregation tries to follow him in a number of other translations, this can be disconcerting to the readers. Although some may enjoy making comparisons, it seems best under those circumstances to use one translation in order to concentrate on the thoughts presented by the preacher. But under other circumstances, it is best to use more than one translation. When one is studying God's Word, using several translations is as good as having that many commentaries to go deeper into a passage. It is always good to assess a translation's dependability as a whole and its faithfulness in each passage. The basis for such an assessment is the concern of our question, "Which translation of the Bible?"

WHO IS QUALIFIED
TO TRANSLATE?
The translator must know the languages

The one who does the work of translating must be a master of the language in which the original is written and an equal master of the language into which he is making the translation. This includes not merely the meaning of words but the significance of how they are put together in grammar and syntax. Each language has its own idioms, and a mechanical rendering of words will not automatically lead one to the proper meaning. A

12

computer, for example, cannot be programmed to assure a good translation. In an experiment cited by the New York Bible Society, one computer was given the task of translating into modern English the well-known statement, "The spirit is willing, but the flesh is weak." The result was, "The liquor is great, but the meat is lousy." The translator cannot be replaced by a computer.

The translator must know the Bible and believe its message

Many object to this criterion. After all, they argue, if a person knows the languages, he should be able to translate the sentences whether he believes them or not. But translation involves many selections of meaning and words. If a person is not aware of the whole context of a passage, or for that matter, the context of the book he is translating, or even the context of the entire Bible, he is unprepared to select the best rendering of one particular sentence. It is important to see the harmony of the whole. If a person rejects the Bible as the Word of God, he may know the contents of Scripture but deny the harmony. He accuses the Bible-believing individual of prejudice for accepting harmony, but he himself is guilty of prejudice in choosing meanings that would be most in keeping with his own beliefs. Granted, one's belief influences his translation, but if his beliefs are wrong, they have an influence in an erroneous direction. It is well to recognize that no one will have a complete knowledge of the Bible, nor have a belief totally commensurate with the perfect understanding of Scripture, but the closer an individual is to this ideal, the better qualified he becomes as a Bible translator. But the further he is steeped in either ignorance of the Bible or disbelief in its message, the more seriously he will be handicapped in rendering its truth effectively.

The translator must communicate the words of life

It is one thing for a person to *understand* the meaning of a passage, and another for him to be able to *convey* this meaning to another person's mind. This demand is an intangible one.

The translator should be able to convery the very mood and feeling of the original, so that the passage gains the desired reaction in the heart of the reader. The *King James Version* has long excelled at conveying the mood and feeling of Scripture. A majestic beauty accompanies its words; a certain awe is awakened, and the reader feels carried along by the faith and devotion of the translators, even though they remain unknown to him. In this area, however, translations come through in different ways to different people. Some appreciate one type of expression and some prefer another. One must make allowance for different tastes in judging the translations.

HOW TO MAKE A BIBLE TRANSLATION
The text

The beginning point for the translator is his use of the text. Many mistakenly picture the New Testament translator poring over ancient Greek manuscripts as he does his work, but actually translators seldom consult the early manuscripts themselves. They depend on the textual scholars for working over the mass of manuscripts and trying to discern which reading most nearly represents the original writing. The results of this labor are published in what is called the Hebrew text of the Old Testament and the Greek text of the New Testament. The text includes not only the reconstruction of the original writing, but also an *apparatus* at the bottom of each page showing how the *witnesses* vary among the leading manuscripts at the points of *variant readings*. In this footnote-summation of evidence (apparatus), not only the readings from individual Greek manuscripts (variant readings) are noted, but also those from the early versions (translations) and quotations from the early fathers (witnesses). At times the possibilities in a variant reading are so evenly divided, combined with other principles of textual criticism, that it is difficult to arrive at a positive decision. The New Testament translator may choose to differ from the decision found in the Greek text he is using, but he does not

Greek text,
Codex Sinaiticus

deal with the manuscripts themselves. He works indirectly through the use of the modern Greek text.[7]

No original autographed writing has been preserved from the hand of a Biblical writer. If one had been, no doubt some would be worshiping the relic rather than the One to whom the Bible leads us. But we have great assurance of knowing what the original said because of the number of copies of the Bible available in ancient manuscripts and the excellent caliber of transcription. No other writing from antiquity has the textual witness that the Bible enjoys. Whereas one could count on the fingers of one hand the classical works that boast as many as a hundred manuscripts, the New Testament numbers its copies of the whole or parts at more than four thousand. Add to this the more than eight thousand in Latin and another thousand in other versions, and the materials become overwhelming.

The accuracy of most of these manuscripts is exceptionally fine. In Old Testament studies, a comparison between the copy of Isaiah found among the Dead Sea Scrolls dating about 100 B.C. and the earliest Masoretic texts from about A.D. 900 indicates to a textual scholar how carefully the Jewish scribes kept these writings. The variant readings are few between the two, although their work was separated by a thousand years.

15

Westcott and Hort were outstanding textual critics who made the following observation after years of study on the New Testament text *(Greek New Testament,* p. 565):

> If comparative trivialities, such as changes of order, the insertion of or omission of the article with proper names, and the like, are set aside, the words in our opinion still subject to doubt can hardly amount to more than a thousandth part of the whole New Testament.

This number of words would occupy one half of one page of the Greek New Testament they were using.

Numerous slight differences are naturally present because of the great number of manuscripts. By community of error in manuscripts, they are grouped according to families and assigned to different places and different times of origin. Handwriting experts assist in dating the origin of each manuscript.

The most highly valued manuscripts—because they are early, dependable, and fairly complete—are the codices *Vaticanus* and *Sinaiticus.* (A *codex* [pl., *codices*] is a manuscript bound together like a book, rather than rolled into a scroll.) Both these early codices were transcribed about A.D. 350. Among the oldest manuscripts of the Greek are the John Rylands fragment of the Gospel of John (c. 125), the Papyrus Bodmer II of John (c. 200), and the Chester Beatty Papyri of the Gospels and Acts, the Pauline Epistles, and Revelation.

Although attempts to standardize the Greek New Testament were made as early as the fourth century, it was not until the time of the reformation movement that a new step was taken. Scholars no longer simply copied manuscripts, but upon the basis of available manuscripts attempted to reconstruct how they felt the original Greek text read. Erasmus introduced the first modern Greek text of the New Testament in 1517. In the middle of the century before, in 1453, the invention of printing had taken place. Now the necessity of handwritten manuscripts ceased, and the printed Greek text formed the basis for the translation of the New Testament. The Roman Catholics, however, still used the Latin Vulgate as the basis for their English translations.

Erasmus' Greek
New Testament

Numerous helps

• *Reference materials.* Reference books and specialists surround the translator as he does his work. The book kept closest at hand is a good Greek-English lexicon, which tells the meanings and usages of the words. Some of these dictionaries specialize in particular periods of the Greek language, such as Classical, New Testament (Hellenistic), or Patristic. Greek grammars are necessary reference works, too. They help to indicate the idioms and shades of meanings from both regular and irregular uses. Parallel grammatical examples add assurance of precise meanings for the passage being translated.

One of the strange circumstances of translating is that the translator must understand the meaning of the passage before he can translate it properly. One might think the translation could be made by use of lexicons and grammars and then the meaning would become clear in the translation. Usually, however, there are different possible directions a translation might go, but to be faithful to the intention of the original author, his precise meaning should be carried in the translation in as clear a way as possible. In actuality, the proper translation procedure requires several steps. The first is a rough translation recognizing the possibilities of the passages. Then when the exact meaning of the section is determined, the final translation will put the proper meaning into the best language to convey that meaning to the reader. This procedure demands the aid of good commentaries to study the meaning of the passage.

• *Special studies.* Studies on translation, on theological points, on historical background, on exegetical principles, on individual passages—all these may bring additional insights as decisions are made how to translate a particular passage.

• *Other translations.* Another helpful aid to Bible translation is to read former translations of the Bible. A translation is the better for the translator's awareness of how the passage has already been translated. The translators of the *King James Version,* for example, made good use of the translations published in the century prior to 1611.

This practice, however, can be both an asset and a liability. Some are too quick to copy what has already been done, and others are too anxious to change to something else for change's sake. A similarity in wording does not necessarily prove one translation used another, especially if that reading is the simple best rendering of the passage. The two translators may have reached the same conclusions independently. Neither should one go to a different wording when he thinks that it has already been expressed in the best known way.

• *Plurality of translators.* Another plus factor in producing a superior translation occurs when more than one person shares in the translation. No matter how accomplished an individual may be, he has his blind spots and his particular views that need testing by other minds. Also, an expression that means one thing to one person may come through with a different meaning to someone else. When a translation is refined by a number of minds, it is likely to be more enduring than the single effort.

• *One translator.* A word might be said on the other side, however, favoring translations by individuals. The individual translator has no need for compromise; he can present his own case clearly and forthrightly. The translation can also preserve the color and freshness contributed by an outstanding personality without its dilution by many other minds. Perhaps it is best to have some individual translations and some by groups of scholars.

• *The experts.* In this day of specialists, it is difficult to find individuals adept in knowledge of the Bible, knowledge of the Greek or Hebrew, and use of the English language. To be safe, the work of the Biblical scholars should be submitted for further refinement by an expert in English. Grammatical slips, awkward phrases, ambiguous expressions, unnecessary words, offensive terms—all tend to clutter the translation of God's Word. This does not mean that the English stylist should alter the content for the sake of eloquence, but the precise level and mood that is found in the Greek should be sought in the English. After the literary adjustment, the results should be reviewed once again by the Biblical linguists to make sure nothing has been lost in the true meaning of the passage.

• *The reader.* Help can also be found in another direction. After all the experts have done their work, still one cannot be sure what the reaction will be from the average reader. It is helpful to know what he appreciates and what he finds objectionable, troublesome, or lacking. By trying the translation on people of different ages and walks of life, the translator can be more certain of a careful choice of expression. He wants to keep it living to as as possible, but always true to the original.

Thus a person is surrounded with a great number of helps while he is poring over the text of the Bible.

Certain principles

Each translation of the Bible has been undertaken with certain guidelines to follow. Those most important to that particular work are usually listed in the preface. Because these principles vary considerably among different works, these will be treated more in later studies of individual translations. At this time, however, it is well to note their importance and list a few of the guidelines.

George Campbell of Aberdeen in 1789 summarized the criteria of good translating under three principles:

1. To give a just representation of the sense of the original.
2. To convey into his version, as much as possible, in a consistency with the genius of the language which he writes, the author's spirit and manner.
3. To take care that the version have, "at least so far the quality of an original performance, as to appear natural and easy."[8]

The first of these is the single principle that cannot be omitted from any treatment of principles of translation. To present faithfully the meaning intended by the author of the original work is the prime task of the translator. Just how this is best accomplished has long been a matter of debate among translators. Some have favored a literal type of translation, especially conscious of giving the meaning in the framework of a word-for-word rendering. The opposite view is known as "free translating." Its advocates insist they are more interested in the content than the form of what they are translating. Campbell's second and third principles listed above reflect an emphasis in the direction of free translation. Retaining the spirit of the author and a natural ease in the translation is difficult to accomplish, especially if one is attempting to follow closely the idiom of another language.

The debate between the literal and the free, as well as further principles, will be discussed in Chapter Four.

HOW TO JUDGE A BIBLE TRANSLATION

A person may say to himself, "I'm not planning to translate the Bible. Why should I be reading about how it's done?" But each person who reads a translation should be able to make an estimate of that translation. What are its strong points? Its weak points? Are there better translations? The more a person knows about the process of translating, including the history of what has been done in the past and what is now available, the better that individual will be able to select the best translation for his reading and study of the Word of God.

Faithful to the original

Again, a person may be saying to himself, "But if I can't read the original Hebrew text or Greek text myself, how can I tell how faithful a translation is to the original?" Since faithfulness to the original is the ultimate test, this is an important question. Even though the average person cannot read the Hebrew or Greek, some steps are still possible for him. Even if one does use the original languages, he will still want to take these additional steps:

• *Read the guidelines,* in the preface or elsewhere, according to which the translation was made. Are the guidelines worthwhile? How well did the translators succeed in following them?

• *Compare the translation* with other translations. Check a free translation against a literal translation, a new translation against an old one. Are the differences changes in meaning or only changes in form? Do the changes in meaning come from new evidence or simply new theology?

• *Check further in the helps* the translators use themselves. Use lexicons, concordances, Bible encyclopedias, and special studies. Look up the commentaries on the passages in question.

• *Study the translators* as well as their translations. They may have written something on the passages they have translated. Just as a book is better understood if the author's viewpoint is known, a change in translation may be understood better by knowing the position of the translator.

Meaningful to the reader

The worth of a translation can also be judged according to its impression on the reader. Does it convey a clear, simple message to him? Does it arouse his interest and stimulate him to read more? Does it inspire trust in the translation and (more importantly) a conviction in the truths written there? Does it lead to faith and action called for by the Word of God?

The answers to these questions will differ concerning the

The Vulgate

same translation, depending on different individuals' feelings. They cannot be the sole basis of judgment for a translation, but they must be included.

Lasting in value

Some translations have proven their value in the past, but does that mean they will always have the same value in the future? Other translations are new, so how can one tell whether their value will endure? Perhaps it is unfair to the new translations, but the verdict of time is of great help as one studies the history of Bible translations. Perhaps one can note the characteristics of those that endure and watch for these marks in the newer translations.

In the chapters that follow, the suggestions outlined here will be pursued further in application to individual translations.

POINTS TO PONDER

1. Why is a translation necessary?

2. Do we need more than one translation?

3. At what times is it best to use only one translation? When is it best to use more than one?

4. Do the beliefs of a translator have anything to do with how good a translation he makes?

5. How can you check on the faithfulness of a translation?

6. What do you look for in a good translation of the Bible?

---

[1]Charles Butterworth, *The Literary Lineage of the King James Bible* (1971), pp. 250ff.

[2]Alexander Campbell, *The Sacred Writings*, p. iii.

[3]John Skilton, ed., *The New Testament Student at Work*, vol. II (1975), pp. 219, 220.

[4]Dewey M. Beegle, *God's Word Into English* (1960), p. ix.

[5]Frederic Kenyon, *Our Bible and the Ancient Manuscripts* (1948), pp. 155-180.

[6]Bruce Metzger, *A Textual Commentary on the Greek New Testament* (1971), p. 198.

[7]See Bruce Metzger, *The Text of the New Testament* (1968).

[8]As cited by Eugene Nida, *Toward a Science of Translating* (1964), pp. 18, 19.

Chapter Two
REVIEWING THE PAST

f a person is serious about selecting a good English translation of the Bible, he has to go back a long way. He needs to trace the whole history of English Bible translation. History is the teacher, and today is its pupil. Today's reader should profit by the trials and attempts of the past and use them to better understand the intentions of today's Bible translators. Some such intentions are to be followed, others avoided.

The Protestant English translation most used today, the *King James Version*, has come from a long three and a half centuries ago. We need to understand its heritage too, in order to appreciate its language.

EARLY ENGLISH TRANSLATIONS
Paraphrases of Caedmon

The translation of the Bible into the English probably has been going on from the earliest stages of the English language. But in those early times there was no full translation of either the Old Testament or the New Testament. Only small sections were transferred to the English, and only a few fragments of

24

these examples of early translations are extant today. The earliest of these originated about A.D. 670, from the mouth of a workman in the abbey of the Lady Hilda at Whitby in Yorkshire, England. His name was Caedmon.

The story is told that Caedmon started his treatment of the Bible because of a dream. In the middle of a party, everyone at his table was asked to sing a song of his own making. Feeling he could not do this, Caedmon left and hid in the stable. When he had fallen asleep, he dreamed that a man insisted he sing about how all these things were first created. He did as the man directed, and when he awoke he remembered everything he had sung in his dream. He later added more verses, and when they were heard by others, the Abbess Hilda urged him to join the brotherhood as a monk. He received instruction about the Bible and in turn rendered many of its stories into Old English poems. He is credited with a metrical version of Genesis, Exodus, and Daniel.

Caedmon's work, however, seems to have been done as paraphrase, not translations. True translation work is of two major types: the literal, word-for-word approach, and the free translation approach, which seeks to present the same sense as the original but not necessarily the same grammatical form or closeness of words. A paraphrase is still more free than a free translation. It restates a passage in the writer's own words with no regard for the form and wording of the original. Even the figures may be altered entirely. A paraphrase is not considered an actual translation, but it at least should convey an impression of ideas from the original.

Caedmon's paraphrases provided a "people's Bible" that could be sung and memorized. Copies of these included Old English poems from other sources. Their Anglo-Saxon vernacular is so strange beside the modern English that one needs a translation even of that text. Here is an example of Moses' address to the desperate Israelites before the crossing of the Red Sea:

No beoth ge thy foshtran, theah the Faraon brothe
swerdwigendra side hergas,
eorla unrim! Him eallum while

mihtig drikten thurh mine hand
to daege thissum daedlean gyfan,
thaet hie lifigende lang ne moton
aegnian mid yrmthum Israbel a cyu.

If we turn this into more recent English line by line, following the word order fairly closely, the result will be something like this:

Be not frightened thereat, though Pharaoh has brought
sword-wielders, vast troops,
men without number! To them all will
the mighty Lord through my hand
this very day a recompense give,
that they may not live long
to frighten with distress Israel's kin.

These lines are a paraphrase of the words of Moses in Exodus 14:13, 14, "Fear ye not, stand still, and see the salvation of the Lord, which he will show to you to day: for the Egyptians whom ye have seen to day, ye shall see them again no more for ever. The Lord shall fight for you, and ye shall hold your peace" (KJV).[1]

Translation by Aldhelm

The earliest translation (not paraphrase) into the English is reported to have been made by Aldhelm, Bishop of Sherborne. He died in 709. The extent of his work was a translation of the book of Psalms. It is even doubtful whether the version of Psalms in the Anglo-Saxon preserved in an eleventh-century manuscript at Paris actually represents his version. The first fifty Psalms are in prose and the rest in verse.

Venerable Bede

The monk of Jarrow, Bede (673-735), was the greatest name in the history of the early English church. Besides writing the *History of the English Church* and commentaries on many books of the Bible in Latin, he also translated the Creed, the Lord's Prayer, and other Scripture into the English tongue. The ac-

26

count of his death, as told by his follower, Cuthbert, has become a classic.

The great scholar had been translating the Gospel of John. On the eve of Ascension Day, 735, he had finished a day of translating and dictating to his students, even though he knew he was dying. He had repeatedly told them to write quickly, for he did not know how much longer he had to live. By evening only one chapter remained untranslated. The next morning a lone youth was ready to continue taking down the translation of the beloved scholar, but the scribe hesitated to press his master further. Bede would not rest. "It is easily done," he said, "take thy pen and write quickly." The day wore on; he was interrupted by farewells to his beloved brothers. His strength was failing, but he struggled to translate the last of John's Gospel. Finally, as light of day was almost gone, his tired and grieving scribe leaned down and whispered, "Master, there is just one sentence more." Bede whispered back, "Write quickly." The scribe wrote on, came to the conclusion, and then said, "See, dear master, it is done now." "Yes," Bede replied, "you speak truly; it is finished now." By his request they laid him on the pavement of his cell and, having repeated the Gloria, with the name of the Holy Spirit on his lips, he breathed his last.[2]

Bede had knowledge of the Latin also some Greek. Perhaps he used not only the Latin Vulgate as the basis of his translation, but the Greek as well. No trace was left of his translation work after the treasures of Northumbria were wiped out by the Danes. Nevertheless, the influence of his accomplishments has been great from this formative period on.

King Alfred is another who encouraged and engaged in Bible translation in the ninth century, but no copy of his work has survived, either.

The Lindisfarne Gospels

Another type of Bible translation dating back to the tenth century is called *interlinear glosses*. One example is a magnificent Latin manuscript of the Gospels made about A.D. 700. Then in about 950 Aldred the priest wrote his Anglo-Saxon word-for-word translation between the lines of the Latin. These "glosses" remain the earliest known version of the Gospels in the English language. They are called "The Lindisfarne Gospels" because the original Latin manuscript had been copied down by Eadfrith, Bishop of Lindisfarne.

Ormulum

Even this early in the history of English translations, one finds the two extremes still in vogue today: the free paraphrase at one end of the spectrum, and the word-for-word literal translation in the interlinear form at the other extreme. In the thirteenth century an Augustinian monk named Oron brought out another paraphrase of parts of the Gospels and Acts. He made this metrical version to be used in church services and included brief explanatory notes. This is known as "The Ormulum" and is preserved in an exceptional manuscript that can be seen in the Bodleian Library at Oxford.

In this period the paraphrase seemed to have more attraction than the literal translation did. For example, Genesis and Exodus were put into verse form for general use.

Shoreham and Rolle

Many changes were converging in England to bring about a whole new period in the history of the English Bible. The Norman conquest in 1066 had brought new influences upon the language of the people. By the 1300's the French of the Normans had blended sufficiently with the old Anglo-Saxon that the English language proper was emerging. This is seen in two of the translations coming from this period. In about 1320 William of Shoreham produced his translation in the Kentish dialect of southern England, and about 1340 Richard Rolle came out with his translation in the Yorkshire dialect of northern England. Each was in English, each was of the book of Psalms, and each was more a translation than a paraphrase.

The stage was being set. Concessions were being made to the common people; to their needs and rights. English literature was appealing to the awakening Englishmen. Langland, Gower, and Chaucer were influential literary figures. Besides this, the people were getting a taste of the Word of God in their

Wycliffe's
English Bible, 1382

own tongue. The circulation of the Psalms stirred their desire for the whole Bible to satisfy their intellectual and spiritual hunger.

THE FIRST ENGLISH BIBLES
Wycliffe's Bible, 1382

The first English translation of the entire Bible is associated with the name of John Wycliffe. No one knows just how much of the Bible was translated by Wycliffe himself, but there is no doubt that he was the moving spirit behind the total work. The time was ripe, and he was the man for the hour.

Certain forces stood opposed to the translation of the Bible. The Roman Catholic insistence that the common man could not understand the Scripture without a priest to explain it to him discouraged the use of the Bible in the language of the people. Furthermore, any opposition to the religious authorities led to the label of heretic, and this would anathematize any work that did not carry the official approval of the ecclesiastical authority.

At that time the political and social orders were so bound up with the Roman Church and the power of the wealthy that any plea for more privileges for the common person was viewed with suspicion. John Wycliffe had already collided with all of these issues before he undertook the translation of the Bible.

Wycliffe had been educated at Oxford and for a short time became master of Balliol College. After he had passed middle age he began taking part in public controversies. In the lecture hall and from the pulpit he denounced the authority of the pope and the role of wealth and power of the Roman Church in civil affairs. He renounced the ecclesiastical canon law in his support of the Scriptures alone. He was anxious to lead the people of the land to an understanding of their rights and repsonsibilities. He wanted them to have the Word of God in their own language, so they could read it in their homes and live it day by day. In 1377 Pope Gregory XI issued five papal bulls attacking him and demanded his imprisonment. But the English government refused to restrain him.

The New Testament was completed by 1380 and the entire Bible by 1382. Wycliffe was then rector of Lutterworth, but he kept in close touch with friends at Oxford and London. These assisted him, no doubt, in his translation work. Nicholas Hereford was largely responsible for translating the Old Testament.

The first edition of the Wycliffite version was extremely literal, especially the work of Nicholas Hereford. It bordered on the type of linear glosses that even followed the word order of the Latin—and this was a translation based on the Latin.

In the same year, 1382, Hereford was summoned to London, where he was excommunicated. He soon dropped out of conflict with the Roman Church. Wycliffe himself was attacked in a sermon preached at St. Mary's at Oxford, and his followers were for the first time labeled "Lollards." A fierce controversy then raged at Oxford. Wycliffe was denounced as a heretic, and he lived out the remaining eighteen months of his life in retirement. This was 1384; in 1428 at the order of Pope Martin V his remains were dug up, burned, and the ashes scattered on the waters of the stream near his home.

The activity of the Lollards and Wycliffe's translator friends did not cease with Wycliffe's death. The Wycliffite Bible was revised. The second edition was not a word-for-word rendition of the Latin and had still greater appeal to the common people of the land. This revision was largely the work of John Purvey, Wycliffe's secretary. Both these versions enjoyed great popularity, as evidenced by the number of manuscripts still remaining of each.

It is noteworthy that these versions were issued before the invention of printing. Not until 1731 was Purvey's New Testament printed, then in 1848 the earlier New Testament, and finally the whole Wycliffite Bible was printed in 1850.

The immediate use of this translation is all the more remarkable for the conditions under which it was circulated by the Lollards. In 1408 the "Constitutions of Oxford" forbade "anyone to translate, or even read, a vernacular version of the Bible in whole or in part without the approval of his diocesan bishop or of a provincial council."[3]

Tyndale's Bible

Between Purvey's revision of the Wycliffite Bible and the making of the next major translation, the world was stirred by one momentous happening after another. The Turks conquered Constantinople, and streams of Greek scholars made their way to the west, bringing with them numerous Greek manuscripts of the Bible. Within a year, Gutenberg printed the first sheets on his newly invented printing press; now the Bible could be run off in hundreds of copies instead of being laboriously copied by hand. Erasmus published the first Greek text of the New Testament based upon the witness of not more than six manuscripts. Martin Luther nailed his ninety-five theses to the door of the church at Wittenberg, and the reformation soon was under way.

The first part of Luther's Bible translation into German was issued in 1522. Earlier, in 1471, an Italian Bible was printed in Venice, and a Dutch one appeared in 1477. A French Bible was printed in Lyons about 1478. Such activity in Bible translation was not found in England just at that time. The "Constitutions of Oxford" did not allow it, and a general fear that reformers would introduce heresy into their translations held translation work in check.

William Tyndale, trained at Oxford and Cambridge, was convinced that the confusion of people's minds could be settled only by the use of the New Testament as the court of appeals in questions of life and doctrine. This meant that the people must have access to the Bible in their own languages.

A dispute between Tyndale and a learned man is included in *Foxe's Book of Martyrs:*

> The learned man said: "We were better be without God's law than the Pope's." Master Tyndall, hearing that, answered him: "I defy the Pope and all his laws"; and said: "If God spare my life, ere many years I will cause a boy that driveth the plough shall know more of the Scripture than thou dost."

Tyndale tried to gain permission to work on his translation of Scripture while living in England, but he failed, so in 1524 Tyndale left for the continent. He had completed his translation of the New Testament and the printing had begun when he was discovered and forced to leave Cologne. In Worms he completed the printing, and within a short time, copies were being smuggled into England.

This is an example of his translation:

> Come vnto me all thee that labour and are laden and I wyll ease you. Take my yooke on you and lerne of me for y am meke and lowly in herte: and ye shall fynde ease vnto your soules for my yooke ys easy and my burthen ys lyght.

Note how closely the later *King James Version* follows its wording. (English spellings were not standardized until centuries later. The first edition of the *King James Version* had spellings similar to these.)

As many copies of the Worms edition as the Bishop of London would locate were collected and ceremonially burned at St. Paul's cross in October of 1526. The authorities in London had even attempted to buy out the issue from the printers in order to destroy them (Tyndale had approved of the transaction in order to finance a revision of his work).

The next nine years were occupied in producing translation work on the Old Testament as well as revisions of the New. Although Tyndale could not return to England, the attitude of the authorities was changing. By 1535 Cromwell and Cranmer were convinced that approval should be given for Bible translation into English. Queen Anne Boleyn accepted the gift of a magnificent copy of Tyndale's new edition. Tyndale was then residing in Antwerp, a free city, where he should have been safe. He was betrayed, however, kidnapped, and taken from the city. After an imprisonment at Vilvorde, Belgium, he was tried as a heretic and in October, 1536, he was strangled and burned at the stake. As he died, he cried out, "Lord, open the King of England's eyes."

Coverdale's Bible, 1535

The cause for which Tyndale had died was indeed turning for the better in England. His New Testament had been violently excluded from its shores, but he had lit the light that would never be extinguished. The very words of his translation were to be incorporated in succeeding works. Cromwell, now Secretary of State, urged Coverdale to publish a complete English translation of the Bible. This was not an official authorization, but the work carried a dedication to Henry VIII and was later printed in England; this was a first. Tyndale had been unable to complete the Old Testament, and in those sections of the Bible after 2 Chronicles, Coverdale was the pioneer translator. In the New Testament he followed Tyndale closely but did replace some of the ecclesiastical terms Tyndale had avoided.

Matthew's Bible, 1537

Now that the gates were open, translations began to come forth one after the other. Matthew's Bible, however, was more a *revision* than a translation. When a work becomes too free to be a translation, it is a paraphrase, and when a work follows closely a former translation, it is a revision rather than a fresh translation. Matthew's Bible follows closely the part of Tyndale's work that had been published and also the part he had completed in manuscript form.

John Rogers was a disciple of Tyndale who worked Tyndale's translations into his complete Bible. For the rest of the Bible he used Coverdale's translation. The name, "Thomas Matthew," however, is given at the bottom of the dedication. It has never been determined whether this is another name for Rogers or the name of an assistant, but it is agreed that the work belongs to John Rogers. Rogers was considered a heretic by the church of England; it is possible that he fabricated the name, "Thomas Matthew," to avoid prejudice against his work. Thus the same translation that had been condemned by Henry VIII and the heads of the church of England in 1525 was in 1537 being sold in England by permission of Henry with the support of the Secretary of State and the Archbishop of Canterbury. This revision included many marginal comments, introductions, chapter summaries, and woodcuts.

The Great Bible, 1539

The Great Bible, 1539-1541

The English Bible had been in the homes, but now it was officially placed in the churches. Cromwell gave the order for Coverdale to make a new revision on the basis of Matthew's Bible. The work was printed on better paper and bound in a volume of large size. In September of 1538 the order was given that a copy should be put in an accessible place in every church in the land. The results were an improvement over what had been produced previously. The people came to the churches to read the Word of God.

Taverner's Bible, 1539

As Coverdale was preparing his first edition of the Great Bible, an Oxford scholar, R. Taverner, was making his own revision of Matthew's Bible. He introduced some helpful changes, particularly in the New Testament portion. It was reprinted once, but never did rival the Great Bible. It gradually dropped from view and was not significant to later translations.

The Geneva Bible, 1557-1560

The precarious conditions in sixteenth-century England continued to influence the course of Bible translation. King Henry VIII had thrown off the bonds of Rome and the pope, but he had also reacted against the principles of the reformation. He did not trust Protestant leaders, whether they were in England or in other lands. Especially after the execution of Cromwell, his resistance was more pronounced. Again Tyndale's translations were ordered destroyed, and Coverdale's New Testament was likewise condemned. The common people were not to read any part of the Bible in public or at home. All notes were to be expunged from other Bibles. Needless to say, this move discouraged both new translations and revisions.

When Edward VI began his reign in 1547, everything changed. In his short period of power forty editions of existing translations were issued—but no new translation.

With Mary Tudor another reversal occurred in favor of Catholicism. The reformers were particular targets, and the ones associated with translation were among those to suffer. Cranmer and Rogers were burned at the stake, and Coverdale narrowly escaped like fate. Copies of the Bible were removed from the churches, and all public reading of the English Bible was ordered to stop.

Many chose to flee from such conditions in England, and

The Geneva Bible, 1560

Geneva was a favorite haven in the storm. Geneva was not only the home of Calvin, but also of Beza, the outstanding Bible scholar of his time. John Knox thought that here was the "most perfect school of Christ" since apostolic days. English exiles gathered here to continue the work of translating and revising. William Whittingham was the leader in this endeavor. The results of their work were published in 1560 in the version known as the Geneva Bible. They took for their basis the Great Bible's Old Testament and Tyndale's last revision of the New. Their notes were outspoken against the papacy and strongly Calvinistic. The Geneva Bible was well received. At first it was published by the English group of Christians in Geneva, but then in England. During the reign of Elizabeth, seventy editions of the Geneva Bible and thirty of Whittingham's New Testament were published. This was the most popular translation used in the homes, while the Great Bible was used in the churches.

The Bishops' Bible, 1568

When Elizabeth succeeded Mary on the throne of England, the English Bible was placed again in the churches. But now deficiencies in the Great Bible were becoming evident because

36

of the presence of the carefully prepared Geneva Bible. Matthew Parker, Archbishop of Canterbury, maintained "yet should it nothing hinder but rather do much good to have diversity of translations and readings."[4] He stated this in defense of reprinting the Geneva Bible, although he himself was pressing ahead with a new version, the Bishops' Bible. This translation was undertaken because the Great Bible was not popular, while the Geneva Bible has sectarian marginal notes and questionable renderings.

Archbishop Parker and eight bishops made a revision of the Great Bible and published their work in 1568. The Bishops' Bible gained considerable acceptance and was placed in the churches, but was not as popular as the Geneva Bible.

The Rheims and Douay Bible, 1582-1609

By now it was evident that English translations were here to stay. They were occupying an important place in the lives of the people. For this reason the heads of the Roman Church decided they should have an English translation of their own representing the Roman point of view. Gregory Martin had left England and founded a college in northeastern France. The New Testament was translated and given the name of the place, Rheims (1582). By the time the Old Testament was translated, the college had moved to Douay, so it was given the name of that place (1609-1610).

This translation was made from Jerome's Latin Vulgate, not from the original Greek and Hebrew. The Romanist Bible did not have as popular a reception as the Protestant ones. Between 1582 and 1750 the New Testament was reprinted only four times, the Old Testament only once. A revision made by Bishop Richard Challoner (1749-1763) was authorized for use by American Roman Catholics (1810) and occupies a place in Catholicism comparable to the *King James Version* among Protestants.

The King James Version, 1611

The scene has now changed in England, from a situation where the people had no Bible in English to the perplexing

37

necessity of choosing from among a number of translations. Some staunchly preferred one, others roundly criticized another.

When King James succeeded Queen Elizabeth in 1603, he called a conference of bishops and Puritan clergy to try to settle differences among them. When the suggestion was given that a new translation be made from the Greek and Hebrew with marginal notes restricted to matters of language and parallel passages, King James immediately approved. He appointed fifty-four of the best scholars to undertake the work. Forty-seven actually participated. They were divided into six groups. From these groups their work went to a committee of twelve, two from each group. Final differences were settled by a general meeting of each group.

Although inaugurated by the throne and carried out by leading church authorities, the *King James Version* did not receive automatic acceptance. It took almost fifty years to achieve a higher place than the popular Geneva Bible. But the excellence of this translation is attested by 350 years of history, as the *King James Version* has held a place of top priority since that time. (The characteristics of this translation will receive fuller treatment in Chapter Five.) Its beauty of language comes from the period of Shakespeare and Milton. Its heartfelt message breathes from a century when translators had given their lives through fire and sword to deliver the Bible to the people. Its faith is manifest in the proposition that these truths being transmitted were the very Word of God.

POINTS TO PONDER

1. What were the earliest attempts to put parts of the Bible into English—translations or paraphrases? What is the difference?

2. Why was it so long before English translations were made of the whole Bible?

3. Were the numerous editions of English Bibles in the 1500's mainly translations or revisions?

4. Why has the *King James Version* remained popular?

[1] As cited in F. F. Bruce, *The English Bible* (1970), pp. 4, 5.
[2] See Ira Price, *The Ancestry of Our English Bible* (1953), p. 227.
[3] F. F. Bruce, p. 21.
[4] Cited in F. F. Bruce, p. 91.

The Gutenberg Bible

Chapter Three
COMING TO THE PRESENT

he *King James Version* had won the day. Both in the home and in the church, this was the translation used in the English-speaking countries. For over two centuries little effort was made to improve it. Only in limited circles and personal endeavor does one find other translation publications between the printing of the King James Bible in 1611 and the first authorized revision in 1881.

BETWEEN THE PAST AND PRESENT
Roman Catholic translations

While Protestants read the *King James Version* and grew in their love for it, Catholic priests did not encourage Bible reading, and considerable dissatisfaction over the Douay Bible developed. Cornelius Nary felt that people did not take pains to read the Douay-Rheims Bible because it was so literal and archaic. In 1718 he published a new version of the New Testament. Then in 1738 a new revised edition of the Rheims New Testament was produced, generally attributed to Richard Challoner and Francis Blyth.

The Rheims-Douay
Bible, 1582-1610

In the nineteenth century a whole procession of Catholic translations was produced. Beginning with Coyne's Bible in 1811, no less than eight versions appeared in the next five years.[1] After the Roman Catholic Emancipation Act, 1829, the number of translations increased still more. In America, Francis Patrick Kenrick published a six-volume revision of the Roman Catholic Bible between 1849 and 1860. Still, the Douay-Rheims-Challoner Bible (1750ff) was the most used version among English-speaking Catholics. This was authorized in 1810 for use among the Roman Catholics of America.

Jewish translations

During this period most English-speaking Jews used the *King James Version* of the Old Testament. There were several attempts at revisions for parts of the Hebrew Scriptures. Benisch, between 1851 and 1856, issued a translation of the whole Hebrew Bible, and Michael Friedlandler released another revision of the King James in 1884.

41

Private revisions and translations

It has been estimated that the two and one-half centuries between the King James and the Revised editions, close to a hundred revisions or translations of the Bible or parts of it were published.[2] Gilbert Wakefield, with Unitarian tendencies, issued a translation of the New Testament published in London in 1791. John Wesley, the founder of Methodism, made a private revision of the *King James Version*, published in 1745 and reissued in succeeding years. It was entitled, *The New Testament with Notes for Plain Unlettered Men Who Know Only Their Mother Tongue*. In 1768 Edward Harwood put out *A Liberal Translation of the New Testament*. His was a startling change from the King James. "Oh, Sir!" exclaims Peter at the transfiguration. "What a delectable residence we might establish here."[3] Anthony Purver brought out a "new and literal" translation in 1764. This became known as "The Quaker Bible."

Henry Alford, Dean of Canterbury, contributed notably to New Testament studies. He published an edition of the Greek New Testament and accompanied it with generous commentary. He also issued a revision of the authorized King James in 1869. He expressed his hope that this revision would soon be replaced by an authoritative revision. The very next year the Convocation of Canterbury began the work that was published as the *English Revised Version* in 1881.

In America, the earliest new translation of the New Testament was issued by Alexander Campbell in 1826. Campbell justified the need for new translations in his preface. A living language is constantly changing, he said, and periodically requires new translations. He also said that the Christian scholar of his day should be better equipped to translate God's Word because of the stock of ancient manuscripts discovered since the time of King James. The growing fund of knowledge of Biblical philosophy, geography, and history further enabled one to recapture the meaning of the original. Furthermore, Campbell raised theological objections to the *King James Version*. He felt that the translators reflected the king's own views of witchcraft, predestination, and related doctrines.[4]

Alexander Campbell's revision, called the *Living Oracles*, was

The King James
Bible, 1611

based upon the work of three British men, Macknight, Doddridge, and George Campbell (no relation). One distinctive characteristic was the translation of *baptizo* as "immerse." This rendering of the word had already been used by Nathaniel Scarlett in his New Testament of 1798. Campbell was also careful to omit ecclesiastical terms he felt were misleading; for example, *assembly* was used for *church* and *favor* for *grace*. He placed the verse numbering in the margin and made use of sense paragraphs rather than marking each verse as a paragraph. His translation is literal and dependable, but the wording weighs heavy because the English natural to his day is unnatural to ours.

Robert Young is best known for his *Analytical Concordance to the Bible*, but he also produced a *Literal Translation of the Bible* (1862). This is an extremely literal, word-for-word translation. If one is looking for an example of a literal translation that not only sounds unnatural but also is difficult to understand, this

43

version provides passage after passage. To use this translation in study as a literal comparison against a free translation is possible, but to read it for devotions is difficult.

Another literal study Bible, issued in England but used in the United States, was translated by Joseph Bryant Rotherham. In 1872 his New Testament first appeared, and between 1897 and 1902 the Old Testament was published. The whole publication was called *The Emphasized Bible*. Rotherham was at first a Wesleyan minister, then a Baptist, and finally a minister of the Disciples. He, too, used the word *immersion* to clarify baptism. His English text is laid out with various signs used to convey detailed shades of meaning and emphasis inherent in the original. This is the basis for the name, *Emphasized Bible*.

The increasing use of recently discovered manuscripts, the printing of new Greek texts by textual scholars, and the growing study of Biblical criticism seem to have influenced a flow of literal translations. B. W. Brameld published a translation of the Gospels in 1870. In this work he claimed to have expunged all spurious passages, bracketed the doubtful ones, and made a complete revision based on the Greek texts of Griesbach, Lachman, Tischendorf, Aldorf, and Tregelles.

Though many new translations and revisions were issued, most people went on using the *King James Version* in all its beauty and majesty.

Major revisions

A revision is different from a translation. The translator is free to select his own words and style, but a reviser must observe more limitation in preserving the style and expression of the work he revises.

The *English Revised Version* was a true revision of the King James. It was undertaken in 1870 when a committee was appointed at the Convocation of Canterbury of the Church of England. Two companies of Hebrew and Greek scholars were formed, regardless of denominational association. The Old Testament section was made up of twenty-seven men, and the New Testament section had a like number. American scholars were invited to share in the work and formed similar com-

The Gospell.

and oyle/and layed him on his beaste/and brought hym to a commen hostery. And dresse hym. And on the morowe when he departed/betoke out two pece/ and gave the to the post and said vnto hi. Take cure of hi/ and whatsoever thou spendest above this/whe I come agayne I will recompens or the. Which nowe off these thre/thynkest thou was neghbour vnto hi that fell into the theves honde? And he answered: he that shewed mercy on hym. Then sayd Jesus vnto hym. Go and do thou lyke wyse.

And fortuned as he went/ that he entred into a certayne toune. And a certayne woman named Martha/ receaved hym into her housse. And this woman had a sister called Mari/whi che sate at Jesus fete/ and herde Jesus preach ynge: Martha was combred about moche ser vynge/ and stode and sayde: Master/ doest thou not care/ that my sister hath leeft me to minister alone? Byd her therfore/ that she helpe me. And Jesus answered/ and sayde vnto her: Martha/ Martha/ thou arte busied/ and troublest thy self/ about many thyngs: verely one ys nedfull. Mary hath chosen her a good parte/ which shall not be taken away from her.

The .xj. Chapter.

And it fortuned as he was prayinge in a cer tayne place/when he ceased/won of his di sciples sayd vnto hi: Master teache vs to praye As Jhon taught his disciples. And he sayd vn to them: When ye praye/ saye: Oure father whi ch arte in heve/ halowed be thy name. Let thy

The first printed English
New Testament, 1525

panies. It was agreed that any suggestions made by the American scholars, but not preferred by the British, would be noted in an appendix. Then after fourteen years the Americans could issue their own work. The British completed their New Testament in 1881 and the Old Testament in 1885.

Westcott and Hort published a Greek New Testament reflecting the textual basis for the new revision. This text differed from the Received Text, associated with the name of Stephanus and used in translating the King James, in 5,788 readings. A comparison of the English, however, between the King James and the Revised shows 36,000 changes. Obviously, then, something more than the text caused the changes in the *English Revised Version*.

Frederic Kenyon divides the changes into three categories:[5] (1) Changes in Text;[6] (2) Changes in Interpretation (more of these occur in the Old Testament); (3) Changes in Language (by far the greatest number of changes are of this class, because of the change of word meanings during the passage of almost 300 years). After analyzing these changes and the comparative merits of these two works from 1611 and 1881, Kenyon gives his judgment: "Both are now essential parts of our heritage and the final verdict must be: the Revised for study, the authorized (King James) for reading."[7]

In 1901 the *American Standard (Revised) Version* was published according to the agreement between the British and American translators. This revision is generally accepted as a careful, literal translation and a more accurate rendering of the Greek than the *King James Version*. Neither the *English Revised Version* nor the *American Standard Version*, however, came anywhere near replacing the *King James Version's* popularity. For most of the people, the King James continued as the favorite translation because of the strength and rhythm of its English.

THE TWENTIETH CENTURY

A new requirement

After the turn of the century, a new fashion became popular. Many people craved the Bible not in the English of an eloquent and timeless quality, but in the vernacular of the very time and place the translation was being made. The everyday speech of the common man became the popular model. Argument was made that the New Testament was not written in a Greek of its own but in the common language of the people, and should be translated the same way to retain its closeness to the individual reader.

At times this argument is carried too far. Slang, vulgar speech, and flippant expressions have been used with the excuse that the original sounded that way. This is not a fair representation of the Biblical books. It is true that the New Testament writings were composed in a way to be understandable to the common man, but it is not in the language one would commonly hear in the streets, either then or now. It is in the living language of the people, but at times it reaches heights of eloquence, such as Romans or Hebrews, and never drops to the level of the vulgar.

Whereas former days had required of its translators a faithfulness to the meaning of the original and a dignified, understandable rendering in the English, now there came the demand for a contemporary style of speech.

Weymouth's translation, 1903

A teacher at Mill Hill School and Fellow of University College, London, Richard F. Weymouth published his new translation in London in 1903. He called it *The New Testament in Modern Speech*. In his preface he listed his intentions: (1) to ascertain the exact meaning of every passage; (2) to consider how it could be most accurately and naturally exhibited in the English of the present day; and (3) to furnish a succinct, compressed running commentary. His list points up the desire to make a translation both modern and free in its language.

This translation went through several printings. The fifth edition, with notes, was made available in 1930, and an American edition was issued in 1943.

Moffatt's translation, 1913

In 1913 James Moffatt issued *The New Testament: A New Translation*. In 1924 the Old Testament came out and in 1935, the whole Bible. He affirms in his preface, "I have attempted to translate the New Testament exactly as one would render any piece of contemporary Hellenistic prose . . . ." It is true that the same rules of grammar should be observed in translating the New Testament as in any other work, but it seems that Moffatt means more than that. Moffatt's views are reflected in his further statement, "But once the translation of the New Testament is freed from the influence of the theory of verbal inspiration, these difficulties [the choice of different meanings for the same word] cease to be so formidable." This puts into words the misgivings that increase as one studies some modern translations. Is there a relationship between the growing number of free translations and the growing denial of verbal or plenary inspiration of the Scripture? There need not be a connection between becoming freer and holding a lower view of inspiration, but when the translator himself makes that statement, as did Moffatt in this particular case, there can be no doubt.

The liberalism of Moffatt shows through in some of his translation decisions as well. In the King James, Matthew 1:16 reads: "And Jacob begat Joseph the husband of Mary, of whom was born Jesus, who is called Christ." At this point Moffatt follows Von Soden's text and gives a reading that appears in only one or two manuscripts against the hundreds of dependable manuscripts that have the sentence as found in the King James. Moffatt reads: "Jacob the father of Joseph, and Joseph (to whom the virgin Mary was betrothed) the father of Jesus, who is called 'Christ'." Joseph is not called the father of Jesus in this passage except in a few remote witnesses probably traceable to one manuscript. But Moffatt chose to put this in his translation text. It is common also for liberal scholars to deny the unity of John's Gospel and the Johannine authorship of the book. They insist that this Gospel has several dislocations of passages. Moffatt held this view, so he printed chapters fifteen and sixteen of John between thirteen and fourteen.

Goodspeed's translation, 1923

Edgar J. Goodspeed was a well-known liberal scholar who taught at the University of Chicago. In 1923 he published *The New Testament, An American Translation*. Then, in 1927, *The Old Testament, An American Translation* was issued by four translators under the editorship of J.M.P. Smith. The combined work was entitled, *The Bible, An American Translation*, appearing in 1931. The preface calls attention to the changing English speech and the rapid advance in learning. Goodspeed saw a need for a new translation that claimed to be "based upon the assured results of modern study, and put in the familiar language of today." When one notes changes in the translation, he must judge for himself whether they are based upon the Greek text, the demands of the English language, or because of a shift in the theological beliefs of the translator and "modern studies."

Montgomery's translation, 1924

Mrs. Helen Barrett Montgomery was an important figure in Northern Baptist circles. In 1921 she was president of its convention. In 1924 she published the Centenary Translation of the

New Testament. She describes her aim in the introduction: "To make a translation chiefly designed for the ordinary reader, intended to remove the veil that a literary or formal translation inevitably puts between the reader of only average education and the meaning of the text."

Williams' translation, 1937

Charles B. Williams was one of the original faculty members of Southwestern Baptist Seminary. His purpose in bringing out a new translation, *The New Testament in the Language of the People,* was to make the Scripture as understandable to the modern reader as the Greek was to the original readers in the first century. He expressed this goal in his foreword:

> Our aim is to make this greatest book in the world readable and understandable by the plain people. . . . In accord with this aim we have used practical and everyday words to replace many technical religious and theological terms. In other words, we have tried to use the words and phrases that are understandable by the farmer and the fisherman, by the carpenter and the cowboy. . . . If these can understand it, it is certain that the scholar, the teacher, the minister, the lawyer, the doctor and all others can.

Verkuyl's translation, 1945

Gerrit Verkuyl lived in Berkeley, California, and when his translation of the New Testament was published in 1945, it appeared under the title, *The Berkeley Version of the New Testament.* For the next fourteen years, a group of twenty scholars under the editorship of Verkuyl worked on a similar translation of the Old Testament. The complete work was put out in 1959 in Grand Rapids, Michigan and London, England. A revised edition of the translation was issued in 1969 under the title, *The Modern Language Bible: The New Berkeley Version in Modern English.* The preface begins:

> This is not just another revision: it is a completely new translation. We have turned to the original languages of both Testaments, assured that "holy men from God spoke as they were carried along by the Holy Spirit." Neither is this a paraphrase, for that leads so readily to the infusion of human thought with divine revelation, to

the confusion of the reader. Instead of paraphrasing, we offer brief notes, related to, but apart from, the inspired writings, to clarify and to give a sharper view of the message.

Despite inconsistencies and unwise devices to distinguish the human and the divine, this is a helpful translation. The translators tried to maintain a balance between *freedom* that makes a passage live and *literalness* that remains close to the original wording. Conservative datings included with the books and the notes are instructive.[8]

Revised Standard Version New Testament, 1946

The publication of the *Revised Standard Version* was authorized by the National Council of Churches in the United States. The New Testament was issued in 1945, the complete RSV Bible in 1952. In 1957 the Apocrypha was added. Then in 1965-66 the RSV Catholic Edition was prepared by the Catholic Biblical Association of Great Britain and edited by two of its members who were later added to the standing RSV Bible Committee. Then in 1971 a second edition of the New Testament was printed. In 1973 the RSV Common Bible was released. This was an attempt to make this version acceptable to Protestants, Roman Catholics, and Eastern Orthodox Catholics alike. Old Testament Apocrypha books are included in the arrangement more familiar to Roman Catholics, but placed between the Testaments.

The original translation work was done by a committee divided into Old and New Testament sections. About nine men were active in the New Testament work and thirteen in the Old. All of them were liberal in their theology and shared with Moffatt his denial of verbal inspiration.

This work does not purport to be a new translation but claims to be a simultaneous revision of the *King James Version* and the *American Standard Version* of 1901, which in turn revised the *English Revised Version* of 1881-85. When the RSV was first issued, the wording was considered free, especially for a revision, but since that time newer translations have gone so much further toward paraphrase that the style of the RSV seems rather

50

staid by comparison. Still the liberalism of the translators shows through, in subtle attacks on the deity of Christ and the harmony of certain prophetic passages (see Chapter Five).

C. Kingsley Williams' New Testament, 1949

Mr. Williams was assistant vice-principal of Achimonta College, Ghana, and formerly vice-principal of Wesley College, Madras. He had a special interest in teaching people whose mother tongue was not English, but wanted to come to a knowledge of English. He rendered the New Testament in a simplified version based on a list of 1500 "fundamental and common words that make up ordinary English speech." It was called, *The New Testament: A New Translation in Plain English*.

Phillips' translation

In 1947 the first of J. B. Phillips' *Letters to Young Churches* came from the press. He had been in charge of a large youth group in London in the days of the World War II blitz. He read to them from the King James, but they did not seem to get much from it. He later explained, "So in a very small and amateur sort of way I began to translate them [Paul's epistles] from the Greek, simply in order that they might understand them."[9] Phillips not only received encouragement from the young people, but when he sent Colossians in his form of translation to C. S. Lewis, he, too, wrote encouragement: "It's like seeing an old picture that's been cleaned. Why don't you go on and do the lot?" And he did. In 1947 he brought out the letters from Romans through Jude; in 1952, the Gospels; in 1955, Acts; in 1957, Revelation; in 1958, *The New Testament in Modern English*; and in 1972, the Revised Edition.

For a time this was the most popular of the translations into modern speech and at the same time was the most free among works characterized as "translations."[10] Where the Authorized Version has, "Salute one another with a holy kiss," Phillips has, "Give one another a hearty handshake all round for my sake" (Romans 16:16). Even if one is able to accept this lively style in the epistles, it is less suited to the Gospels, and Phillips fails to adjust.

E. V. Rieu: The Gospels (1952)

In the same year that J. B. Phillips' *The Gospels* came out, the Penguin Classics printed *The Four Gospels,* translated by the general editor, E. V. Rieu. Dr. Rieu had already established a reputation as a lucid translator of Homer. He was a classical scholar. It is interesting to hear the observations given in an interview with J. B. Phillips, E. V. Rieu, and a representative of the BBC broadcasting studio. Dr. Rieu made this statement concerning the Gospels:

> Then again we have to consider whom they were written for. I came to the conclusion very soon that they were written, not for the man in the street, whose existence I do not really believe in, but for the man in the congregation, and that we must not write down to him, that he will not thank us for writing down to him.
>
> To sum up, the Greek Gospels are unique, both in their spiritual content and as works of literary art. They are majestic, and I think we must strive to convey this effect in the best contemporary English at our command and never write down.
>
> The word paraphrase is much misused, by the way; it is often used as a term of abuse for very good translation. I should put it in this way, that it is permissible only where literal translation is liable to obscure the original meaning. I would go further and say that on such occasions it is not only permissible, but it is imperative and therefore it becomes good translation, and the word 'paraphrase' should disappear. [11]

Dr. Rieu's translation of the Gospels is generally accepted as a careful rendering of the original. He has, however, altered the conventional order of the Gospels and put Mark first. This arrangement reflects the unproven theory that Mark wrote first and Matthew and Luke used him extensively in the composition of their narratives.

C. H. Rieu, son of E. V. Rieu, added the translation of Acts to the Penguin series, but the series has gone no further.

The Amplified Bible, 1965

Years of extensive research resulted in the publication of a work that included more than a word-for-word translation. It listed various shades of meaning possible for each important word in a passage, it included clarifying words and comments not actually expressed in the original, and it used italics to point out words not in the original. The Lockman Foundation and Zondervan Publishing House issued the *Amplified Bible* in 1965 after parts of it had been published earlier. Francis E. Sievert was the Research Secretary. The version is a good study Bible, but the numerous markings and additional words make it difficult for public or devotional reading. This is an example (John 3:16):

> For God so greatly loved *and* dearly prized the world that He [even] gave up His only-begotten ("unique") Son, so that whoever believes in (trusts, clings to, relies on) Him shall not perish—come to destruction, be lost—but have eternal (everlasting) life.

Good News Bible (Today's English Version)

The New Testament of this translation was published in 1966. It was also known by the title, *Good News for Modern Man*. The whole Bible was issued ten years later. This version was prepared by the American Bible Society for people who speak English as their mother tongue or as an acquired language. Dr. Robert C. Bratcher led in the translation work, assisted by other members of the Society staff and by a Consultative Committee. The purpose was to publish a popular edition of the Bible that would be contemporary in language, not timeless, and would produce "dynamic equivalence." In other words, the same effect is to be produced on the modern reader today as was felt by the earliest readers. The format is popular, and the pages include line drawings by Mlle. Annie Vallotton. (The fifth chapter will treat this version more fully.)

The New Testament of the GNB has sold over sixty million copies since first published. It is claimed that this is the best-selling Bible translation in history.

The New English Bible, 1970

In Britain a new translation was begun. It was officially authorized, undertaken by a panel of scholars, and intended for the use of persons from every walk of life, but suitable for reading in the services of the church. In October of 1946 a recommendation was approved by representatives from the Church of England, the Church of Scotland, and the Methodist, Baptist, and Congregational churches. They wanted a "completely new translation" rather than a revision, and they instructed "that the translators should be free to employ a contemporary idiom rather than reproduce the traditional 'Biblical' English."

A Joint Committee appointed four panels of scholars in the areas of Old Testament, Apocrypha, New Testament, and Literary Advisers. The names C. H. Dodd, Godfrey Driver, and W. D. McHardy are prominent in the work. The New Testament was completed in 1961, and the whole Bible was published in 1970.

This version was extensively advertised and its sales went quickly into the millions. It has been criticized for its literary style, its textual basis, its theological viewpoint, and its tendency to paraphrase (see Chapter Five for fuller treatment), but this is a major work that will be used for many years to come.

New American Standard Bible, 1971

The foreword to this translation states:

> The New American Standard Bible has been produced with the conviction that the words of Scripture as originally penned in the Hebrew and Greek were inspired by God. Since they are the eternal Word of God, the Holy Scriptures speak with fresh power to each generation, to give wisdom that leads to salvation, that men may serve God to the glory of Christ.

Although fifty-eight scholars worked for more than a decade on this version, only the name of the Lockman Foundation appears with its publication. One of the aims of the translation was to give the Lord Jesus Christ His proper place and avoid detracting from that place, so no name of the translators has been included.

Their first aim was to remain true to the original Hebrew and Greek, in an attempt to produce a literal, word-for-word translation. This version shows less departure from the original languages in formal equivalence than any of the other modern Bibles examined.

Another aim, however, was to make the work grammatically correct in contemporary English. At times the translation had to be adjusted to a more current English idiom than the Greek wording would suggest. In such cases the more literal rendering is included in the margin.

The remaining aim was that this translation be understandable to the masses. To do this, the translators made generous use of marginal notations.

Although this work bears a similar name to the *American Standard Version* of 1901, it claims to be more than a revision. The name is used because of admiration for the work of the 1901 revision and a desire to perpetuate its aims by using the same principles followed in the parent translation (treated more fully in Chapter Five).

The New International Version, 1978

Like the *New American Standard Bible,* this version was undertaken by men who held a high view of Biblical inspiration. After meetings and conferences, committees were appointed for the work, and in 1967, under the sponsorship of the New York Bible Society International, the translating actually began. The translation teams, assigned to individual books, had five men each—two translators, two consultants, and one English expert. Work from these teams went to the Intermediate Committee, then to the General Editorial Committee, and finally to the top Committee on Bible Translation. Each time the work would be gone over word for word and the translation would be further refined. Over a hundred scholars have shared in this work. They represent a great number of church groups, not only in the United States but in Great Britain, New Zealand, Canada, and Australia as well. The New Testament was published in 1973 and the entire Bible in 1978.

One principle held before the translators was the need to put the truths of Scripture into expressions used and understood today. This was to be a contemporary translation, but not a colloquial translation, short-lived and appreciated by only a limited group. It was to be beautiful enough to inspire respect when read from the pulpit—simple enough to be clear to the young person, interesting enough to attract the non-Christian, and meaningful enough to stir the soul of the devotional reader. The leading principle, however, was expressed: "At every point the translation shall be faithful to the Word of God as represented by the most accurate text of the original languages of Scripture."

This is not a word-for-word translation. It attempts to retain the freshness of God's living Word in a free-flowing expression (treated more fully in Chapter Five).

New King James Version, 1982

Thomas Nelson and Sons held the copyright for the *American Standard Version* (1901). As the ASV copyright expired, this publisher also held the copyright for the *Revised Standard Version* (1952). In 1969 the American division of Nelson's Publishers changed hands and its new president, Sam Moore, directed his attention toward more conservative enterprises. The *King James Version* was still the best seller among all the translations, but with the flood of new translations it would never occupy the same place it had known for centuries. For a number of reasons it was time to update the King James, and Sam Moore was among those who determined to do so.

Translators commissioned to undertake the work of revision faced a difficult task: 1) to retain the basic beauty and majestic cadence of the King James translation, 2) to put into clear, contemporary wording the true meaning of the original and 3) to draw this meaning from the Hebrew and Greek texts faithful to that written by the inspired authors and preserved through the ages.

Considerable changes were made. Archaic words and forms were replaced with expressions clear to today's preacher. The Old English "thee," "thou," and "thy" became simply "you" and "your;" old verb endings were altered; punctuation was updated. All of the examples listed in Chapter Five (p. 87) under the weaknesses of the *King James Version* (1611) have been rectified.

New features were introduced to increase the value of the revision. The use of quotation marks makes it easier to follow the dialog. Paragraph headings assist the topical flow. Pronouns referring to God, Jesus, or the Holy Spirit were capitalized. Footnotes were added to clarify the alternatives or give grounds for a translation.

Despite the familiar sound of the old King James still heard in the *New King James,* more changes have been made than one might realize from a superficial reading. Even then one could wish for still more improvements and, on the other hand, might question some of the innovations (for further assessment, see Chapter Five).

The most severe criticism of this work has developed in an arena beyond the sight of the average reader. It has to do with the Greek text used for the translation of the New Testament (more so than the Hebrew of the Old Testament). This problem will be described on page 68f. The decision was given to use the same Greek text as was used in the time of King James throughout the body of the translation (see p. 122).

NEW ROMAN CATHOLIC TRANSLATIONS

Just as the Protestants had shown a growing reluctance to be confined to the King James translation, so the Roman Catholics experienced a desire for something more than their standard English translation, the Douay-Rheims-Challoner version.

The Confraternity Version (New American Bible), 1970

In 1941 a revision of the Rheims-Challoner New Testament was published in the United States under the title *The New Testament of our Lord and Savior Jesus Christ.* This was a major revision bordering on a new translation. The language was modernized, an improved text of the Latin Vulgate as well as Greek readings were consulted, and explanatory notes were included.

After the publication of the New Testament, work on the Old Testament was begun. This was not a revision but a new translation, based on the original Hebrew text. In 1948 the publication began with Genesis and the rest of the publication appeared in four volumes: I, Genesis-Ruth, 1952; III, Sapiential or Wisdom Books, 1955; IV, Prophetic Books, 1961; and II, Samuel-Maccabees, 1969. By that time, however, it was felt necessary to revise the New Testament portion using the Greek text as a basis of translation, and again the Old Testament was revised for consistency. The resulting publication was no longer called the Confraternity Version but rather the *New American Bible*. It was published in 1970 as the work of fifty-nine Catholic scholars and a few Protestant consultants. The flavor of "Bible English" preserved in the earlier Confraternity edition had been abandoned and a thoroughly twentieth-century idiom was pursued.

The Westminster Version

English Roman Catholic scholars undertook an independent project of translating the Bible under the general editorship of Cuthbert Lattey, S.J. The New Testament was completed by 1935, and in the same year, the Old Testament started coming out. Lattey died in 1954.

R. A. Knox's version, 1950

This translation was made official for use in Great Britain. Monsignor Ronald A. Knox worked through the years to produce this version "translated from the Vulgate in the light of the Hebrew and Greek." It has been welcomed by Catholics everywhere and used to some extent by non-Catholics as well. The New Testament appeared in 1944 and the Old Testament, in two volumes, in 1949 and 1950. Knox also wrote a helpful book, *On Englishing the Bible* (1949), in which he describes the trials of a Bible translator.

The Jerusalem Bible, 1966

Outstanding among Catholic scholars was Marie-Joseph Lagrange, a French Dominican. He led in establishing a small school in Jerusalem, L'Ecole Biblique. This was at the beginning of the century. Now the institution has become recognized throughout the world as a center of Biblical studies and related subjects, such as archeology. As they pursued Biblical research there, the Catholic scholars determined that the translating of the Scriptures in light of the latest progress in Biblical learning would be the height of achievement. So a French translation was made of the Scriptures, issued in forty-three fascicles between 1948 and 1955. In this *Bible de Jerusalem* were included explanatory notes, introductions to the individual books of the Bible, and a system of cross references. In 1956 this was published in one volume and soon became the most used of the French versions.

By 1957 work was under way to render the achievement of this French version into the English. Alexander Jones was the eminent Catholic scholar who led the work. This was not a mere translation of the French into English, but the original languages and texts were used for translation and the notes and commentaries were updated. The work was published in 1966. Its objectives were set down:

> To serve two pressing needs facing the church, the need to keep abreast of the time and the need to deepen theological thought. This double program was carried out by translating the ancient texts into the language we use today, and by providing notes to the texts which were neither sectarian nor superficial.

The scholarship reflected in the notes is of the liberal school of thought that would deny that Moses wrote the Pentateuch or that Peter wrote 2 Peter. Whether Catholicism has actually been kept out of the notes and translations or not (see Chapter Five), this translation is widely used by Catholics and Protestants. It is one of the major English translations and will be influencing people for many generations.

OTHER WORKS
The Living Bible, Paraphrased, 1971

Kenneth Taylor decided he needed the Bible in a form that would be interesting, understandable, and convincing for his children. So he began putting the Bible into his own words for use in their family devotions. This led to the first publication of his paraphrases—*Living Letters* in 1962. Then in succession he issued *Living Prophecies* (1956), *Living Gospels* (1966), *Living Psalms and Proverbs* (1967), *Living Lessons of Life and Love* (1968), *Living Books of Moses* (1969), and *Living History of Israel* (1970). Then in 1971 the Tyndale House Publishers of Wheaton, Illinois, published the first printing of *The Living Bible* in its entirety. Before the year was over three more printings were needed. Billy Graham added his recommendation and by the end of the next year two million copies had been sold. By now Taylor's work had gone through many hands—"under the careful scrutiny of a team of Greek and Hebrew experts to check content and of English critics for style."

The Living Bible is a paraphrase. What does this mean? In the preface to the work, this explanation was given: "To paraphrase is to say something in different words than the author used. It is a restatement of an author's thoughts, using different words than he did."

One danger of reading a paraphrase is that people forget they are not reading a translation. A related danger is that still wider choices are left to a paraphraser than to a translator. Any step in the wrong direction may lead still further into error when put into the paraphraser's own words (this is treated more fully in Chapter Five). Different reactions have resulted from the widespread use of *The Living Bible*. Some have emphasized that more people are reading the Bible because of the interesting style; some give testimony that they have come to the Lord through reading the pages of this paraphrase. Others emphasize the extreme familiarity usually characteristic of a paraphrase, which tends to cheapen the Word of God. *The Living Bible* with its "Barney the Preacher" (Acts 4:36) is not as wayward as some, such as *The Cotton Patch Version*. The ultimate question with a paraphrase, as with a translation, is whether the meaning of the original is actually conveyed to the mind of the reader (see Chapter Five).

The Authentic New Testament

The Jewish scholar, Hugh J. Schonfield, claims that former translations of the New Testament are defective. "What we have been accustomed to reading is largely idealized interpretation created by various schools of Christian faith and piety."[12] He set out to produce the authentic version with his own understanding of Jewish backgrounds and diversity of styles. When one remembers that Dr. Schonfield, in his *Passover Plot*, reconstructs the crucifixion of Jesus as a deliberate hoax to establish his longed-for messiahship, one questions the trustworthiness of Schonfield for an "authentic" pronouncement in translation. He has attempted to depart from conventional uses in translation. He avoids the words *baptism, church, apostle, bishop, deacon,* and in their place he has *immersion, community, envoy, supervisor, administrator.* His translation as a whole is not that different, however. He does put the books in different order, gives titles to these groups, and adds notes of introduction.

New World Translation

This is a translation produced by the Jehovah's Witnesses and clearly reflects their doctrine.

Barclay's New Testament

This has been published in two volumes: *The Gospels and the Acts of the Apostles* (1968) and *The Letters and the Revelation* (1969). Barclay always communicates with stimulating thoughts. His translation has the same effect. He also includes a forty-five page Appendix to Volume I, "On Translating the New Testament."

Others

There are too many translations even to be cited in as brief a study as this. Individuals have made translations; for example, Beck's *New Testament in the Language of Today* (1963) and Wuest's *Expanded Translation* (1956ff). There are translations in series; for example, *The Anchor Bible.*

Numerous attempts have been made to abbreviate the Bible. These are some of the recent ones: *The Narrative Bible* (Enslow, Hillside, NJ) allows four and one-half pages for Job and just two for Galatians. It is described as "condensed for easy reading." *The Compact Bible* (Oak Tree, Amboy, WA) is cut short by one-third. *Reader's Digest* condensed the Bible by 40% in its *Reader's Digest Bible*. Although highly publicized, this was no new translation. The *Revised Standard Version* was used and chapters and verses snipped away. Chapter and verse numbers were omitted, so one has difficulty determining what has been left out.

Frequent attempts have been made to simplify the Bible. Two of them are *The Simple English Bible* (New York) and *The Bible in Basic English* (Cambridge). The latter limits itself to a 1,000-word vocabulary of which 850 words are considered basic.

In 1982 the Jewish Publication Society of America completed its project translating *The Holy Scriptures*. It had published its work by sections in 1962 (Torah), 1978 (Prophets), and finally the completed publication (with the Writings). Prior to this time a publication of 1917, based upon the *King James Version*, had provided the standard Jewish translation. The new work, however, was heralded as fresh, understandable, and contemporary, without the use of any past Christian translations.

For a list of New English translations, paraphrases, and revisions published between 1881 and 1973, see John H. Skilton, "The Study of Modern English Versions of the New Testament," in *The New Testament Student at Work*, Presbyterian and Reformed Publishing Co., 1975. For a bibliography including reviews of the important contemporary translations, see Jack Lewis, *The English Bible from KJV to NIV* (1981), pp. 367-408.

POINTS TO PONDER

1. What is new about translations of the twentieth century?

2. How many translations have you used of those listed in this chapter? How many would you like to become acquainted with? Why?

3. How can translations contribute to your Christian life?

4. Does every Bible translation have something worthwhile to contribute?

---

[1] See G. MacGregor, *A Literary History of the Bible* (1968), p. 245.
[2] Ira Price, *The Ancestry of Our English Bible* (1953), p. 279.

[3]Cited in MacGregor, p. 252

[4]Alexander Campbell, *The Christian Baptist* (1825), pp. 259, 260.

[5]Frederick Kenyon, *Our Bible and the Ancient Manuscripts* (1948), pp. 238-242.

[6]Kenyon gives convenient lists on pp. 17, 39, 247-256.

[7]Kenyon, p. 244.

[8]See F. F. Bruce, *The English Bible* (1970), pp. 229-233

[9]See E. H. Robertson, *The New Translation of the Bible* (1959), p. 121.

[10]S. L. Greenslade, ed., *The Cambridge History of the Bible,* vol. III (1965), p. 376.

[11]E. H. Robertson, pp. 125, 126.

[12]See E. H. Robertson, p. 166.

Chapter Four

VIEWING THE STANDARDS

t's easy to read."
"I can understand it."
These reasons are frequently given for liking a translation. As important as these reasons are, they do not form a strong enough basis to make a good selection. One needs to include all the ABC's of Bible selection: Accuracy, Beauty, and Clarity. Although it might be better to give *clarity* second place in the listing instead of putting it after *beauty*, any reasonable arrangement must list *accuracy* first.

ACCURACY

A clear, easy-to-read translation is not necessarily a good translation. Even if it pleases both the literary expert and the contemporary tastes of the modern reader, such recommendations are not sufficient to assure a good translation. The test of *accuracy* is necessary before all else. Does the translation faithfully convey the meaning intended by the original author? Unless a translation is accurate, it does not matter how beautiful it sounds or how vivid its language is—the translation has failed. The words may be clear in giving the ideas of the translator, but if his ideas are not faithful in representing the work of the original author, then the translation has missed the mark. Accuracy is the first standard used to measure the success of a translation.

In what ways can a translation be "accurate"?

Aspects of translation accuracy

• *Formal Detail.* One can approach accuracy as a constraint to make as many details in the translation match the original as possible. This constraint might be directed toward word equivalence. If the word is a noun in the Greek, find an equivalent noun for the translation. If the noun comes after the verb in the Hebrew, make the noun come after the verb in the English. This detailed accuracy may not be simply in the area of grammar. The figures used, such as sheep, drachma, crown, in the original, will be retained in detailed accuracy as sheep, drachma, crown, in the translation.

• *Essential message.* When the translator realizes that his main concern is to convey the meaning from one language to another, then the element of message becomes fully as important as any individual detail. Perhaps the reader is in a land that has no sheep, and these animals are unknown to him. Will the translator try to make the message clear by sacrificing detail and using another animal in translating *sheep*, or is that *too* free? Perhaps a *drachma* is no longer a coin used for money. Will he sacrifice detail and substitute the nearest coin of money that is in use among the readers of his translation? Perhaps the Greek word for *crown* means the victor's crown in an athletic contest and not the royal crown of a king. Will he give several words in the English translation to make this clear, or will he leave that for the commentary? Accuracy requires a balance of detail and message to insure that the right meaning comes through. But what is the proper balance of detail and message? Some translators might sacrifice so much detail that here, too, the message loses out.

• *Proper spirit.* More intangible is the spirit of a passage. A good translation will not only duplicate the detail and message, but also the precise *feeling* of the original writing. If these words come in love, if these words are given in rebuke, if these commands are issued in authority—whatever spirit permeates the original, this same aura should be felt in the translation.

- *Corresponding naturalness.* Particularly difficult for a translation is to capture the same natural flow of the original writing. It is not fair to represent a vibrant, moving message in the Greek or Hebrew with a flat, wooden translation in the English. The accuracy in detail must be balanced with natural, flowing English in order to maintain an accuracy of the whole. To do this, it is impossible to translate word for word or preserve a foreign word order.

- *Reader reaction.* Every passage in Scripture was written for a purpose and with a desired reaction from the reader. It is part of the duty of the translator to attempt to inspire in his reader the same response expected by the original work. It should be neither more nor less startling than the language of the inspired writer.

- *Preferred text.* Formal detailed accuracy requires the use of the most accurate Greek or Hebrew text as the basis for the translation. For most English readers, much of this work takes place behind the scenes. Textual scholars are constantly attempting to decide, for example, what Paul actually wrote in that autographed original of his letter to the Romans. Copies were made of this letter, then copies were made of the copies, and the chain so continued down through the ages. The scribes were not inspired, and, naturally, mistakes and corrections crept in with the passage of time. Some variations were intentional, but most were purely accidental. In either case, it is necessary to separate the changes from the correct readings carried in the original writings. Since no original autographed copy of any Scripture is in existence today, it is very difficult at times to reconstruct the correct, original wording. This accounts for some differences in translations. Modern translations make high claims for superiority in this area, because many more manuscripts are known today than were used in the making of the *King James Version.* Today's judgment is better because we have more information, is the claim.

Considerable debate has been building up at this point,

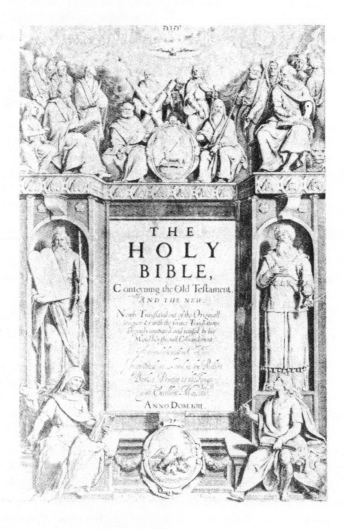

The King James Bible

however. Defenders of the *King James Version* point out that the few manuscripts used in forming the basis of the King James translation represent the very readings found in the vast majority of manuscripts, most of which date from the Middle Ages. Some call this the Majority Text. When the Revised edition was brought out in 1881, however, the Greek text of Westcott and Hort was available in proof sheets. These two scholars strongly followed the testimony of two manuscripts, Vaticanus and Sinaiticus (the codices mentioned in Chapter One), and when these two agreed in a reading contrary to the majority of manuscripts, the two were preferred. These two manuscripts were earlier than the hundreds of the Majority Text that came from the Middle Ages. They thought the earlier manuscripts should be preferred since more time allows more opportunity for corrupting the text with mistakes. Opponents answered, however, that false readings appeared early in the manuscripts, but the true renderings won out in the later copies.

The Majority Text advocates claim that the only reason we have Vaticanus and Sinaiticus in such a good state of preservation is that they were so filled with mistakes they were retired from use. To the contrary, however, it is pointed out that more recently discovered papyri manuscripts tend to corroborate the readings in Vaticanus and Sinaiticus. To this the advocates of the Majority Text reply that these papyri manuscripts come from the same locality as Sinaiticus and Vaticanus and probably had the same line of descent in their copies, which explains their similar readings.

Also, the defenders of the *Textus Receptus* (similar to the Majority Text) raise the question, "How do you explain the high degree of agreement in the majority of the later manuscripts if they do not have the original reading?" To this, the Westcott and Hort position suggests that in the fourth century an effort was made to standardize the text, and that after this time most scribes followed the line of readings that was agreed upon. This agreement, however, was inferior to some of the earlier witnesses, which were closer to the original and less corrupted in differences. So the discussion rages.

In the final analysis it appears that Westcott and Hort did

give too much weight to Sinaiticus and Vaticanus when they stood almost alone against all other testimony (for example, the ending of Mark) but that on the whole the earlier manuscripts are to be respected in the majority of their readings.

Since Westcott and Hort's time other Greek texts have been produced, such as Nestle's (a combination of B. Weiss, Tischendorf, and Westcott and Hort) and the Bible Society Text (Aland, Metzger, et. al.), and a new text has been produced to represent the view of the Majority Text school (Arthur L. Farstad and Zance C. Hodges, eds., *The Greek New Testament Majority Text* [Nelson, 1982]; see also Wilbur N. Pickering, *The Identity of the New Testament Text* [Nelson, 1977]). A nineteenth-century work by F.H.A. Scrivener is the last to publish Stephanus' text of 1550 as compared with the readings found in half a dozen other Greek texts, but the witness of more recently discovered manuscripts is not listed.

Which reading to accept in a given passage involves more than the weight of one manuscript or the counting of any number of manuscripts. The matter of context is most important. Which meaning seems most likely to fit the meaning of the passage and the author's own characteristics? The reading that best explains the existence of all other readings is also of value in determining the right one.

A decision necessary at the outset is whether the difference is deliberate on the part of the scribe, or accidental. Many of the rules drawn up by textual critics apply only if the change made by the scribe was made deliberately. At times the reason for a change is impossible to determine.

A person should not become discouraged concerning the difficulties in establishing a pure text. If he cannot read Greek or Hebrew, he can compare the *King James Version* with the *American Standard* (either the 1901 edition or the *New American Standard* of 1971); he will find little difference required by different preferred texts. A list of the hundred major passages that are in question in the Gospels and Acts can be found in Appendix I of Frederic Kenyon's book, *Our Bible and the Ancient Manuscripts* (pp. 247-256). A handy volume containing a list of disputed passages and their readings is *A Textual Commentary on the Greek*

New Testament (1971) by Bruce M. Metzger. The ending of Mark (16:9-20), the woman taken in adultery (John 7:53—8:11), the confession of the Ethiopian eunuch (Acts 8:37), and the trinity passage (1 John 5:7) are among the questioned passages that should be checked in the different translations.

Whether literal or free

The main differences among translations exist not because of a difference in text, but because the type of translation work is either literal or free. One might feel that a translation must be literal in order to be accurate, but this is not always true.

For example, the word for "sit down" in the Greek is made up of two words that, taken literally, would mean "fall up." Even the rendering "sit down" is rather misleading. When we think of sitting down, we usually think of sitting upright in a chair. But when the people of New Testament times sat down at a formal meal, they did not sit in a chair but reclined on a couch. For this reason some translations try to convey a more accurate picture by rendering the word "recline." At Luke 11:37 the King James translates the word "sat down to meat," but the *New International Version* renders the word "reclined at the table." In any event, more than one word is used in the English to translate just one word in the Greek.

No translation can be completely literal and at the same time convey the meaning accurately. Rather than a *word-for-word* translation, it is more important to have a *sense-for-sense* rendering. Jerome recognized this priority.[1] On the other hand, once it is established that a strict word-for-word translation is impossible, some go to an extreme in rebelling against the formal details. It is one thing to resort to free rendering when it is necessary, and another to alter the original at will, putting the translator's ideas across rather than the author's message.

The interlinear volume with its Greek on one line and the English below is the most literal type of New Testament translation. This may be helpful for study, but the loss is great in naturalness, impact, and even in the basic meaning of the passage. At the other extreme, the most free of the works becomes a paraphrase rather than a translation.

Whether translation or paraphrase

Drawing the line between a translation and a paraphrase is frequently difficult. Some translations are accused of lapsing into paraphrase when they become extremely free. Others maintain that freedom is necessary when there is no other way to convey the meaning. In this case the work should not be considered a paraphrase but a translation, even though it is put in language far from the formal details of the original.

Paraphrases are designed to put the Scripture into the idea framework of the one who is making the transfer from one language to another. A paraphrase does not purport to be a translation. An example of one is *The Living Bible, Paraphrased.*

To make a comparison of literal translation, free translation, and paraphrase, let us consider a variety of renderings of 1 Kings 20:11. The *King James Version* represents an older, literal translation: "Let not him that girdeth on his harness boast himself as he that putteth it off." This is clearer in the *New American Standard Bible,* also a literal translation: "Let not him who girds on his armor boast like him who takes it off." The *Jerusalem Bible* is an example of a free translation: "The man who puts on his armor is not the one who can boast, but the man who takes it off." The *New English Bible* is supposed to be a free translation, but is accused of being a paraphrase at many points. This is how it renders the same passage: "The lame must not think himself a match for the nimble" (a possible Mishnaic development of meaning; the Greek of the LXX[3 Kings 21:11] has what could literally be translated, "Let not him who is crooked boast like him who is straight"). *The Living Bible* gives the paraphrase of the same passage: "Don't count your chickens before they hatch!" One can readily see that the paraphrase is easy to understand, but rather difficult to identify with the saying in the original. Further confusion could arise when a coming generation insists that the saying, "Don't count your chickens before they hatch," comes straight from the Old Testament, along with chapter and verse from 1 Kings, *Living Bible.*

The degree of accuracy is not determined by whether a translation is literal or free, but by how well it conveys the meaning of the original. It should retain the formal details as far as possible and still carry the message, with the spirit of the passage preserved and an impact on the reader similar to that intended by the original author.

Each translation must be measured by such standards as these. The paraphrase should not be considered a translation; it is more like a minister's sermon about the Bible than the Bible itself.

BEAUTY
How does it read?

When one judges a translation by the criterion of beauty, the results must be subjective. What is beautiful to one person may be disagreeable to another. What is appreciated in one age may be unacceptable in another. What is popular in one circle of society may be shunned by another. One must expect to find various reactions to the same translation; still, one cannot deny the place of this standard of beauty. Each individual should acknowledge whether a particular translation is easy for him to read, holds his interest, and leaves him with a sense of having read the Word of God.

Some translators downgrade the beauty of the original of the Bible, but there is no justification for this. Some parts have higher literary quality than others, but each has its own beauty and character. Paul is an example of versatility. He can write with such power and urgency that the language can scarcely keep up with him, as in Galatians. Or he can rise to the heights of eloquence, as in 1 Corinthians 13. No matter what the style of a passage, a translation should reflect the literary quality of the original.

How does it sound?

The many uses of the Bible should be remembered. Some reading is done in the privacy of one's home, but other important reading is done as a part of the worship of the church, the preacher's sermon, and the scholar's study.[2] How does the translation sound when it is read aloud? As a person works at translating the Scriptures, he soon learns that a necessary step in checking his translation is to read it aloud and see how it sounds.

Some translations are ill-suited for the worship service. One wonders, when this is the case, whether such a translation is a faithful rendering of the original. Paul wrote his epistles to be read in the worship service. His style and language were appropriate to the occasion. A translation should likewise fill the need for delivering God's Word, whether in corporate worship, Bible study, personal evangelism, or private devotions.

The *King James Version* excels in this area of beauty. This translation has been so firmly established in the hearts of Christian worshipers that it has become the standard for beauty of expression identified with Biblical language. Some, however, question the advisability of identifying one's faith with archaic language. It is better to keep God's Word living and vital with a breath of freshness, they say. On this point the judgment is subjective; what is best for one may not be best for another. At least one should recognize the range of tastes in this area. Although one may not be able to capture the majestic beauty and moving cadence of the King James expressions, other translations can also possess a degree of dignity and naturalness while carrying God's message to the hearts of believers.

How does it look?

The format of a translation can also contribute to its beauty. The style of type that is used, the paper, the margins, the number of columns per page—all this has its part in the degree of acceptance a translation has in the eye of the reader. One seldom realizes how the layout of a page can tire a reader and discourage his continuing.

The *King James Version* was ordinarily printed with the verses divided into new paragraphs at each verse. The *New American Standard Bible* still follows this format. Although this allows individual verses to be found easily for public reading, it also tends to chop up the sweeping narrative a person enjoys in devotional reading. The presence of verse numbers in the line of the text also tends to stop the eye. With the verse numbers placed in the margin, the text is less encumbered. On the other hand, some translations have a verse number only at the beginning of long paragraph divisions and leave the other verses unnumbered. This makes it very difficult to locate a passage by verse.

When we judge the beauty of a printed translation, we must not forget to consider its physical appearance and format.

CLARITY
It is easy to understand?

Helping a reader understand the meaning of a piece of writing is what translation is all about. Here is one of the disadvantages of the *King James Version.* Although its language is beautiful and its presentation of the gospel is awe-inspiring, its Renaissance English style is not always easy to understand. The best in translation is given in simple words, familiar language, and clear ideas. This requires an idiomatic use of the English, just as the Scripture is written in idiomatic use of the Greek and Hebrew. If one must read a passage over and over again to grasp what is being said, it may be the fault of the translation. Try another translation at that point and see if it makes the passage clearer.

A note of warning must be given at this point, however. The Bible is the Word of God, and one must expect parts of this Book to go beyond the depth of man's understanding. These passages must be rendered faithfully and simply, but the truth is not preserved if one attempts to make shallow the deep places of the Word. A translation cannot guarantee to make every passage of Scripture easily understood, but it must present with clarity what the original author intended to say.

Does it instruct?

The helpful information aiding a person's understanding of the text need not be restricted to additional notes. Some can be given in the very way a passage is translated. A casual reader of the Bible might fail to recognize what business a "publican" was in, but when this is translated "tax collector," it instructs. One may wonder about a "husbandman," but the translation "farmer" is much clearer. The customs, weights, and measures can be given in terms familiar to our experience.

One of the rules of translation observed frequently in the past is the rule of consistency: If a word was translated one way in a passage, then it must be translated that same way throughout the passage. In fact, some words were kept consistent in translation throughout the whole Bible. Many translations today have departed from this practice. A variety of words used to render a single word in the Greek or Hebrew, it is thought, will instruct the reader as to different shades of meaning inherent in the original word. The only trouble with this practice is that the reader is usually unaware that one word in the original is being rendered in different ways in the translation. This is one more reason to compare different translations. Some versions observe consistency of rendering while others give variety of meaning.

To observe how one is instructed as he reads a translation is another test of its value.

Is it precise?

Can the reader see more than one possible meaning in a translated passage? If so, this can be bad. The translator has a fear of allowing the intended meaning to be confused by other possible interpretations. A translation filled with ambiguities, then, is a definite sign of weakness.

In one area this problem is more complicated. What if the passage in the Greek of the New Testament has language that can be taken in more than one way? After all, in every language there will be words that have more than one meaning. One school of thought maintains that the passage should be translated allowing just as many possible interpretations in the translation as exist in the original. Others, however, maintain that the translator should choose one interpretation, make this crystal clear, and exclude the other possible interpretations in order to help the reader. Such a policy places grave responsibility on the shoulders of the translator. A modified practice is to retain the alternative interpretations where the least uncertainty remains, and rule out other possibilities only where it is absolutely clear which interpretation was intended in the original. At times the author may have deliberately chosen his expression to include more than one meaning. When Jesus told Nicodemus he must be born "again" (John 3:3), a word is used in John that means not only "again" but also "from above." Although it is clear that Nicodemus took Jesus to mean "again," it may well be that the alternate meaning of the Greek has its significance also.

A clear translation will keep out all unncessary ambiguities but retain (if possible) the significant ones.

Is it contemporary?

Must a translation be given in the language of its own day before it can have clarity? Some would prefer that the Bible be kept different from other books in its form of expression. They prefer the classical Biblical way of putting things—identified with the *King James Version*. Still others are not as interested in the literary aspect as the theological. Certain words have gathered theological significance through the years and to change them might be to change the doctrine. Since, however, the New Testament was written in a contemporary Greek and not in a classical or special Biblical Greek, it should be translated into a contemporary English. This is part of the requirement of accuracy (translating with the same natural flow as the original) and it also contributes to the understandability. If a translation has archaic words that themselves need explaining, it has not completely translated the message from another time and language. One answer to this need is the recent revision of the King James. Thomas Nelson Publishers has sponsored the work of one hundred thirty men in order to update the wording of the King James, but to retain its beauty and degree of literalness.

This is not to say that every contemporary translation is a good one. Some pride themselves in employing colloquial expressions. Language restricted to usage in limited circles of society, or especially identified with certain times and places, can outdate a work as soon as it is published. Nor does colloquial or trite language suitably express the Biblical message. A vulgar presentation of what is said is especially inappropriate. A translation *can* be contemporary and understandable, but dignified. One must keep in mind the wide reading audience of the Word of God—young and old, rich and poor, educated and uneducated, Christian and non-Christian.

DANGERS
Role of belief

Each person has his own beliefs. These beliefs are bound to influence his judgments to some degree. If a person claims to be entirely unbiased, he is either fooling himself or trying to fool others. Hort believed that the early scribes were saints who did not allow their theological beliefs to influence the readings they copied into the Scriptures. Dewey M. Beegle, in his book *God's Word Into English,* criticizes Hort for his naive attitude, and it may be that this criticism is justified. The irony of the criticism is that Beegle does the same thing for modern tranaslators that he accused Westcott and Hort of doing for the ancient scribes. Neither the ancient scribes nor the modern translators can make decisions without being influenced by their beliefs.

If a person accepts the infallibility of Scriptures, that they are a true and accurate record of what actually happened, that they are inspired by God and are therefore assured of trustworthiness in the originals, he will approach the translation of God's Word with an expectation of harmony throughout its parts. This is looked upon as a lamentable prejudice by those who deny the infallibility of the Bible. On the other hand, the denial of infallibility becomes a prejudice in the opposite direction. In one translation the Bible-believing individual will tend to find harmony, and in another translation the liberal scholar will tend to find disharmony. If a man denies predictive prophecy, it is understandable that he renders the Hebrew of the Old Testament as differently as the wording allows from its fulfillment recorded in the New. Some complain that this is dishonest, but actually the liberal scholar is being honest to his own position as he uses the choices he feels he must to further his own views.

Some would point out that in passages in Titus and 2 Peter the expression of the deity of Christ has been strengthened by renderings even in liberal translations. What many do not realize is that even here the strong affirmation of deity is used to serve a purpose. The liberal translator ordinarily denies that Paul wrote Titus and that Peter wrote 2 Peter. He points to the very language deifying Jesus as an indication of the later date of these epistles when Paul and Peter could not have written them.

If our beliefs are going to influence our translations, then it is important that the beliefs of the translator be in accord with the teaching of the Scriptures. Objectivity is a worthy goal, and we want sincerely to treat the facts as they are and to render a translation that faithfully presents the original text. Truth has no fear in the face of objectivity. But the objectivity of man has its limitations, and that is why it is important to trust oneself into the hands of the translator who has proper starting points—an acceptance of Christ as the Son of God, and respect for the Scriptures as the very Word of God.

Risk of the free

Growing interest in free translations is one of the present trends in Bible translation, but free translations have not just now arrived to replace the literal. Jerome's Vulgate was a sense translation, not word-for-word. Early attempts at putting the Bible into English were more paraphrastic than literal. The *King James Version* itself was a pleasant combination of the literal and free expressions of its own day.

One must recognize, however, the dangers that accompany the free translation. The freer a translation becomes, the more possibility there is for the ideas of the translator to be read into the passage. Even though these ideas may not be in the Biblical text itself, they can be woven into a free, loose translation. One has double trouble, then, when greater freedom in translation is joined with denial of Biblical doctrines by liberal theologians. When the "liberals" produce free translations, the risk becomes greater that their views will be included in the results of their translation work.

On the other side of the question, the individual who has high regard for the inspiration of Scripture is interested even in the smallest detail of God's inspired Word. In fact, he is anxious to duplicate each detail as far as possible in his translation work so that the person who cannot treat the original itself will have as close a facsimile as possible to work with. The literal translations of our own day are produced for the most part by conservative, Bible believing scholars.

It is wrong, however, to conclude that all free translations are made by "liberals." A good case can be made for the desirability of the free translation, but it is a powerful tool and must be guarded closely. The literal method can also be abused, leading to a type of allegorical meaning attributed to the very number and form of the words employed, but neglecting the real meaning of the passage.

The free translation can be put to good use, more readily conveying an accurate impression of the true message. One must be aware, however, of the risks both in the literal and the free methods.

The obstacle of ignorance

A. D. Nock stated in a class at Harvard that if an individual of the twentieth century could live for just one ordinary mid-first-century day with an ordinary family in Jerusalem, he would know more about their life and times than if he studied all the histories on that period available today. We have mountains of studies about the days of Christ and the early church. We also have dreadful gaps in our knowledge, and the small, commonplace things that would help us better understand the language of the New Testament are withheld from us by the stretches of time and civilizations. Numerous difficulties attributed to the Bible and its language are not the Bible's fault, but that of our own lack of knowledge.

The translator of the Scripture will profit by the growing understanding of Biblical times, but he will always be handicapped by ignorance.

SAFEGUARDS

Translators build safeguards into a translation in order to protect their own integrity and provide information enabling a reader to exercise his own judgment on special issues. They supply reasons for their decision to make a change or give a rendering out of the ordinary. They set down principles and explain procedures, passing along to the reader their basis of judgment and aids to understanding. The safeguards appear in different forms in different translations, and must be considered whenever we attempt to estimate the total worth of a translation.

In addition to those provided by the translators, the reader should employ his own safeguards. He is responsible to ascertain the truth provided in God's Word and determine the faithfulness of men in communicating this truth to others.

Preface

• *Explanation.* Each translation provides some word of explanation at the beginning of the work to show how this translation came into being. The textual basis of this work, the type of translation attempted, the particular need this translation seeks to supply—all this should be explained in the preface. The reader must decide, *How real is the need for this translation? Does it actually meet that need?*

• *Claims.* The preface will say something about the principles of translation especially respected by that particular translation. The reader must determine, *Are the principles sound? How well does the translation apply them? Has something important been left out?*

The preface is a safeguard both for the translator and the reader. If one understands the preface, he will be better able to judge the translation.

Annotations

• *Footnotes.* The value of a translation is greatly increased by its footnotes. In fact, some have said, "We don't need more new translations—we need a good *old* one with better footnotes to inform us. The new translations will correct some old mistakes

80

and make some new mistakes of their own." Frequently a change has been made in a translation, but it goes unnoticed unless a note tells what the change is and why it was made.

Some object that the increase of notes has only to do with formal detail and is of little help in getting the message across. Others feel that the use of notes clutters up the page and discourages the easy flowing reading in an avid search for spiritual food. Since the time of Tyndale, some have objected against notes because a person's particular doctrine might easily be written into them.

In any event, notes are an excellent safeguard used to explain the decisions of the translator and to inform the reader.

• *Italics*. Footnotes are not the only devices used to inform the reader. Translators of the *King James Version* were careful to italicize all English words that lacked Greek or Hebrew equivalents in the original. The translators felt that these words were necessary to make the language acceptable and understandable, but they were anxious to be faithful to the principles of a literal translation and wanted to warn the reader when anything was added. This practice has been ridiculed by some today because italics are frequently understood to indicate *emphasis*, rather than the lack of an equivalent word in the original language. Usually, however, those who criticize this practice are strong advocates of a free translation and prefer that the added words, being so many, go unnoticed. Rather than devise some new scheme to inform the reader, they let him remain ignorant of what is being added. The *New International Version* is an exception; it is a free translation, but it indicates additions by enclosing the words in half brackets. The *New American Standard Bible* still uses the italics.

• *Introductions*. Whole books have been written as companions to particular translations. It is valuable to study these books and pamphlets to learn of the principles followed in specific works. Not only does one learn of that translation, but also of the problems and materials of translation work in general. An example of such an introduction is *Good News for Everyone*, written by Eugene Nida to explain the decisions made in producing the Good News Bible.

Tests

• *Compare the versions.* This is a good safeguard the average reader can use. Keep a literal translation at hand for detailed accuracy. Compare a free translation with it to see if the message is the same. If it is different, compare other free translations with the literal translation. Does a pattern develop in which some translations prove to be more trustworthy than others? Do not form a conclusion ahead of time; be certain to check many instances.

• *Check the passages.* Each person should make his own list of those Scriptures he finds significant to compare. The following passages can form the basis for such a list: Isaiah 7:14 (Matthew 1:23), Hebrews 1:1-4, John 1:1, 3:16, the ending of Mark, Genesis 12:7 (Galatians 3:16), Genesis 12:3 (Galatians 3:8), Psalm 51:5, and Matthew 16:18.

• *Verify the interpretation.* Further study of a translation can be done by looking up any doubtful passages in a trusted commentary. Perhaps the new translation has brought to light the meaning that was there all along; a commentary can help as a safeguard to warn against the unlikely interpretation and to corroborate the truth. But even here the commentaries need testing just as the translations do. When one comes to the Bible with faith in Christ as the Son of God, and with acceptance of the Scriptures as the inspired Word of God, his efforts to understand the will of God will be rewarded.

POINTS TO PONDER

1. What are the ABC's of translation selection?

2. What dangers tend to threaten the production of a pure, accurate translation?

3. What are some safeguards that help a person understand and assess a translation?

4. What are key passages you would like to examine in each translation?

5. Which is better, a literal translation or a free translation?

[1] Letter 57 to Pammachius, "On the Best Method of Translating," as cited in Eugene Nida, *Toward a Science of Translating* (1964), p. 13.

[2] See "The Use of the Bible" in *The Cambridge History of the Bible* (1963), vol. III, pp. 479-494.

[3] See W. Schwarz, *Principles and Problems of Biblical Translation* (1970), pp. v ff.

Chapter Five

MAKING A JUDGMENT

ne needs to read more than one translation of the Bible. The Scriptures in their original writings were inspired, but the translations are not. No translation is perfect. A person may have his favorite translation, but his understanding increases when he reads the same truths put in a slightly different way. If nothing more is gained after using a second or third translation, the reader may return to his favorite with still greater appreciation for what he finds there. He may discover other translations he prefers more than the one to which he has been accustomed. Hopefully, a greater knowledge of the different translations available will lead to more Bible reading, a better understanding of God's will, and a life filled with faith and response to God's direction.

The choice of a Bible translation is important. A basis of selection has been set down in the preceding chapters, and now examples will be given as to how a few of the more important translations can be assessed. Each Bible reader must do this for himself. The following judgments listed are only one person's opinion. Each person is responsible for doing his own reading and drawing his own conclusions. These same criteria can and should be used on other translations as well.

The author is reluctant simply to give labels of *excellent, good, fair,* and *poor* in such categories as *accuracy, beauty,* and *clarity,* but it is impossible to set down a more detailed assessment in as short a study as this. Rather than conclude the study with no concrete results, it seems best to give frank conclusions that have been reached by the use of considerations described in the preceding chapters. The reader is not asked to agree with the estimates, but to "walk circumspectly" in his own selection of a Bible translation.

One may question the wisdom of going any further with an estimate if a translation does not measure up in the area of accuracy. After all, if the work does not faithfully represent the Word of God, of what value is beauty or clarity in translation? Hopefully, many readers share and admire that feeling. Many, however, have already used different translations of the Bible and drawn their own conclusions in the areas of beauty and clarity, but have not stopped to think about accuracy. To put accuracy in proper perspective, it is well to recognize the other categories in an independent way, but not to allow them first place in the criteria. Then, too, each of the translations under consideration here shows some measure of accuracy. The Lord can be known through truths expressed in each of them; the way of salvation can be learned.

Weaknesses are emphasized more than strengths in the following estimates. An attempt would be made to balance this out if space allowed. It was felt that the reader could easily find reason for the favorable impressions, but that some justification should be given for indicating weaknesses. At the same time these estimates provide the reader with the type of detail he should include in coming to his own conclusions.

KJV King James Version (Authorized Version)

TRANSLATOR(S) Forty-seven men divided into six groups. Inaugurated by King James, carried out by leading church authorities and scholars.

DATE 1611

PUBLISHER Robert Barker, Printer to the Kings most Excellent Majestie. Many editions; Cambridge, 1629, 1638; Oxford, 1769.

TEXTUAL BASIS Textus Receptus (Beza, 1604)

TYPE OF TRANSLATION New translation with constant use of earlier translations, so it could be considered a revision. Literal, but idiomatic enough to render good English.

ACCURACY

Good. As a literal translation, its observance of details helps the rating of accuracy. The fact that earlier manuscripts have been discovered since 1611 does not render the KJV unsatisfactory, since the differences are not that great and the KJV is extremely faithful to the text then available. Italics inform the reader when words that do not have an equivalent in the Hebrew or Greek are added in the English. One passage, 1 John 5:7, is a later Latin addition that should not be included in the text.

BEAUTY

Excellent. Although beauty in language is somewhat dependent upon each individual's judgment, one must recognize the time-tested preference for the majestic expression and cadence of this translation.

CLARITY

Often unsatisfactory. Not only are many words obsolete or now different in meaning, but some passages are unnecessarily obscured; for example, 2 Corinthians 10:15, 16.

THEOLOGICAL BACKGROUND

Church of England and Puritan theology of the seventeenth century.

WEAKNESSES

Obsolete words

Carriages (Acts 21:15) means *baggage*.
Scrip (Mark 6:8) means *wallet* or *bag*.
Fetched a compass (Acts 28:13) means *sailed around*.

Change of meaning

Letteth (2 Thessalonians 2:7) means *restrains*.
Prevent (1 Thessalonians 4:15) means *precede*.
Charger (Mark 6:25) means *platter*.
Conversation (James 3:13) means *conduct*.

Grammar

Were (Hebrews 5:8) should be *was*.
Whom (Mark 8:27) should be *who*.

Inconsistency

Jeremiah, Jeremias, and *Jeremy* are used for the same name.

Areopagus and *Mars Hill* are used for the same place (Acts 17:19, 22).

Hell is used for both *Hades* and *Gehenna* (*Hades:* Matthew 11:23; 16:18; *Gehenna:* Matthew 5:22; 23:33).

Anachronism

Easter is used for *Passover* (Acts 12:4).

Candle is used for *lamp* (Luke 15:8).

Faulty translation

Second Corinthians 5:14 should not end with a conditional statement.

Doctrinal influence

Be converted (passive) should be *turn again* (active) in Acts 3:19.

Such as should be saved (Acts 2:47) should be *those who were being saved.*

SAFEGUARDS

Italics are used to designate words appearing in translation but having no equivalent in the Greek or Hebrew. A lengthy introduction was included with early editions but seldom accompanies publication today.

New American Standard Bible

TRANSLATOR(S) Fifty-eight scholars sponsored by the Lockman Foundation.

DATE 1971

PUBLISHER Foundation Press Publications, publisher for the Lockman Foundation. Since published by Regal Books, Moody Press, Creation House, and others.

TEXTUAL BASIS Kittel's *Biblia Hebraica;* Nestle's *Greek New Testament,* 23rd edition.

TYPE OF TRANSLATION References describe the NASB both as a revision of the *American Standard Version* (1901) and as a fresh translation based upon the ASV. A literal translation.

ACCURACY

Excellent. A twofold purpose is expressed in the foreword: "to adhere as closely as possible to the original languages of the Holy Scriptures and to make the translation in a fluent and readable style according to the current English usage." The overall accuracy of the translation is high because of the balance of closeness to the original and good expression in the English to convey the true meaning of the original.

BEAUTY

Fair. Of necessity a literal translation cannot achieve the literary naturalness that a free translation can. The NASB makes clear the intention to give careful distinction in translating the tenses of the Greek verbs. This in itself results in an unnatural straining at the tenses in the English. The overall dignity of the work compensates somewhat for the staid results in reaching for the literal.

CLARITY

Good. It is much more clear than the *King James Version*, but remaining literal still restrains the translator from adding words to clarify a passage further.

THEOLOGICAL BACKGROUND

Evangelical. Each translator shared the conviction expressed in the foreword "that the words of Scripture as originally penned in the Hebrew and Greek were inspired by God."

WEAKNESSES

Overtranslation

In Luke's prologue, the Greek word used in verse 1:3 is variously rendered in other translations: *in order, connected narrative, ordered account,* or *in orderly fashion.* The NASB translates it *in consecutive order. Consecutive* suggests chronological order. Luke apparently does not have all the events in chronological order, and the NASB by overtranslating the word makes a claim that may well be contrary to fact.

Overconsistency

The rule of consistency in Greek-English translation has to do with rendering a Greek word consistently by the same English word. Slavish observance of this rule leads to some inferior renderings. Hebrews 9:15ff is as example. The author of Hebrews has been emphasizing that Jesus is the mediator of a better covenant (8:6). But the Greek word for *covenant* also has the meaning of *will* or *testament* (it is the same word as in the title of the Old and New *Testaments*). The NASB translators had been consistently rendering the word *covenant*. In 9:15, however, the point is made that in order to come into effect, a will (testament) requires the death of the one who made it. This is neatly stated in the King James: "For where a testament is, there must also of necessity be the death of the testator." The NASB's use of the word *covenant* at this point ruins the thrust of the argument. *The New English Bible* handles the problem cleverly as a free translation: "he is the mediator of a new covenant, or testament . . .". It is better to abandon the consistency rule if context demands, as it does in Hebrew 9:16.

Lack of harmony

In Galatians 3:16 the NASB renders Paul's statement: "Now the promises were spoken to Abraham and to his seed. He does not say, 'And to seeds,' as referring to many, but rather to one, 'and to your seed,' that is, Christ." When one turns to Genesis 12:7 (or 13:15) in the NASB, he finds the Hebrew rendered, "and the Lord appeared to Abraham and said, 'To your descendants [*seed*, in the margin] I will give this land.' " But the plural *descendants* is just what Paul said it was not (grammatically plural in form). The English word *seed* is a good equivalent translation for the original Hebrew word because either the word in the English or in the Hebrew is singular in form but can be taken for either singular or plural in meaning. The NASB would have done well to stay with *seed* in the Old Testament as well as using it in the New (and in Genesis 22:18).

Preferences

Thee and *thou* have been retained in the prayers to Deity. This practice perpetuates the idea of a separate "prayer language," which the Greek and Hebrew do not uphold.

SAFEGUARDS

The NASB is a good study Bible. The notes are put in the side margin, and a great many parallel and similar passages are noted there as well. Concordance and maps are available in certain reference editions. The literal translation provides the basis for solid Biblical studies.

New English Bible

TRANSLATOR(S)	Joint Committee and four panels under the leadership of C. H. Dodd, Godfrey Driver, and W. D. McHardy. Inaugurated by Church of England, Church of Scotland, Methodist, Baptist, and Congregational churches.
DATE	1970
PUBLISHER	Oxford and Cambridge University Presses, England.
TEXTUAL BASIS	Kittel's *Biblia Hebraica* (third edition, 1937). R.V.G. Tasker, *The Greek New Testament being the text translated in the New English Bible 1961* (Oxford and Cambridge, 1964). L. H. Brockington, *The Hebrew Text of the Old Testament, The Readings Adopted by the Translators of the New English Bible* (1973).
TYPE OF TRANSLATION	New free translation. ''The translators should be free to employ a contemporary idiom rather than reproduce the traditional 'biblical' English . . . a

rendering which should harvest the gains of recent biblical scholarship" (preface).

ACCURACY
Fair. The NEB's freedom in translation often becomes a paraphrase.[1] It introduces many speculative changes that have not necessarily clarified the original message.[2]

BEAUTY
Fair. One is carried by its flow of language. Some English experts, however, such as T. S. Eliot, have criticized it as an example of the decadence of the English language in the middle of the twentieth century. The format is pleasing.

CLARITY
Good. The ideas are put in an understandable way. Occasionally the British idiom obscures the translation for Americans. *Good* refers only to readability and does not consider the faithfulness to the original. The latter is the area of accuracy.

THEOLOGICAL BACKGROUND
Liberal.

WEAKNESSES
Words inserted without grounds
"*Guardian* angel" (Acts 12:15)
"You are Peter, *the Rock*" (Matthew 16:18)

Words omitted without grounds
"Every inspired scripture" [of God] (2 Timothy 3:16)
"A mighty wind that swept over" instead of Spirit [of God] (Genesis 1:2)

Prophecy made inharmonious with fulfillment

"They have hacked off my hands and feet" (Psalm 22:16) instead of "they pierced my hands and my feet" (NASB)

"All the families on earth will pray to be blessed as you are blessed" (Genesis 12:3) instead of "and in you all the families of the earth shall be blessed" (NASB); cf. Galatians 3:8

"A young woman is with child . . ." (Isaiah 7:14), cf. "The virgin will conceive . . ." (Matthew 1:23)

Weakened prophecy

Genesis 3:15: "between your brood and hers" (Makes impossible the reference to Christ which is possible in the Hebrew singular [English, "seed"])

Isaiah 9:6: "in purpose wonderful, in battle God-like, Father for all time, Prince of peace" instead of "Wonderful, Counselor, The mighty God, The everlasting Father, The Prince of Peace" (KJV)

Objectionable renderings

"I never sponged upon you" (2 Corinthians 12:13)

"Once upon a time . . ." (Genesis 11:1)

"This is the story of the making of heaven and earth . . ." (Genesis 2:4)

"This is more than we can stomach" (John 6:60)

"I shall remain at Ephesus until Whitsuntide" (1 Corinthians 16:8)

"You must have nothing to do with loose livers" (1 Corinthians 5:9)

Interpretation but not translation

"Partner in celibacy" (1 Corinthians 7:36) for "virgin daughter"

"It was the eve of Passover, about noon" (John 19:14) instead of "it was the day of preparation for the Passover, it was about the sixth hour"(NASB)

"On the Saturday night" (Acts 20:7) instead of "on the first day of the week" (NASB)

Unfamiliar terms

"So they fell foul of him" (Mark 6:3)

"It is not put under the meal-tub" (Matthew 5:15)

SAFEGUARDS

The NEB translators have published two volumes explaining the texts (Hebrew and Greek) they have used (see above under *Textual Basis*).

They supply a limited preface and notes to explain their purposes and procedures.

RSV Revised Standard Version

TRANSLATOR(S) A group of thirty-two scholars composed the American Standard Bible Committee under the auspices of the National Council of Churches. Luther A. Weigle was the chairman.

DATE 1952

PUBLISHER Thomas Nelson & Sons

TYPE OF TRANSLATION A revision. This was to supply the

need for a thorough revision of 1901, which will stay as close to the Tyndale-King James tradition as it can in the light of our present knowledge of the Hebrew and Greek texts and their meaning on one hand, and our present understanding of the English on the other (preface, p. iv.).

The results, however, must be considered "free," going beyond what the Committee claimed to be doing.[3] The RSV is especially free as a revision, but compared to some modern-speech free translations, it is quite restrained.

ACCURACY

Deficient in vital areas. The translators depart from the Hebrew text (O.T.) to make conjectural renderings wihout inserting any note.[4] F. F. Bruce concluded that the RSV has "blurred some of the finer distinctions in New Testament wording which, while they are of little importance to the general reader, have some significance for those who are concerned with the more accurate interpretation of the text."[5]

BEAUTY

Fair. Once again it is emphasized that this is a subjective judgment. Compared with the trite language of some modern speech, the RSV is beautiful. The translators conscientiously attempted to preserve a dignity making this version suitable for pulpit reading. But even if one does not choose to use the *King James Version* as a standard for beauty, the RSV suffers by restricting itself as a revision of the *King James Version,* and the result is not natural enough to establish its own style of beauty.

CLARITY

Good. The translators' primary goal was to make the translation understandable, and they reached a measure of success in this area. Even here there is room for improvement. What is a *refractory* slave (Titus 2:9)? Does *ablutions* (Hebrews 6:2) make *baptisms* (KJV) more understandable? *Elemental spirits* (Galatians 4:3) is no improvement over *elements of the world* (KJV) and looks in the wrong direction for meaning.

THEOLOGICAL BACKGROUND

Liberal.

WEAKNESSES

Prophecy made inharmonious with fulfillment

Isaiah 7:14—*young woman,* and Matthew 1:23—*virgin*

Genesis 12:7—*descendants* (plural, with no possibility of

being singular) and Galatians 3:16—*offspring* (singular in form and content, with a possibility of plural generic use in other instances)

Genesis 12:3—*bless themselves*, and Galatians 3:8—*be blessed*

Psalm 2:7—*You are my son* (human) and Hebrews 1:5—*Thou art my Son* (divine; see below for explanation)

Psalm 45:6—*Your divine throne* (human) and Hebrews 1:8—*Thy throne, O God* (see below)

Testimony to the deity of Christ weakened

To accommodate our living language *thou, thee,* and *thy* have been replaced by *you* and *your* except in language addressed to God, where the Old English forms are retained. Since this difference does not exist in the Greek, this necessitated an interpretation on the part of the translators each time these pronouns refer to Jesus. Was He considered human or divine? At what point did His followers recognize His divine sonship? By this device a belief in the divinity of Christ is denied of Peter in his good confession (Matthew 16:16), denied of the disciples just before His ascension, denied of Saul on the road to Damascus (Acts 9:5), denied of the prophetic claims (see above). One of the translators, Clarence T. Craig, defended the RSV's position thus: "Would you have the disciples, described by evangelists as without understanding, speak as if they at that time ascribed deity to Christ? When we come to passages in which the faith of a disciple is fully established, the *Revised Standard Version* is unequivocable in using exactly the form which you demand." When one checks the RSV, however, he finds that the translators deny the deity of Christ in the beliefs of His disciples throughout His earthly ministry—despite the words of Thomas, "My Lord and my God" (John 20:28).[6]

The opening of Hebrews is another example of translation that weakens the presentation of Christ. Hebrews 1:2 speaks of God's Son, and most translations render it *his Son,* but the RSV gives *a Son,* which is possible from the Greek but ill-suited to the context. In Hebrews 1:3 the word *reflects* is used to describe Christ and the glory of God. This suggests indirect light, but the Greek word denotes the direct radiance of the light itself.

Popular theories written into the translation

The liberal theologian ordinarily denies the Davidic author-ship of Psalm 51. Whereas the NASB renders verse 18, *Build the walls of Jerusalem,* the RSV reads, *rebuild the walls of Jerusalem.* This latter rendering fits the liberals' theory of its authorship in the Maccabean period of reconstruction, but there is nothing about rebuilding in the Hebrew text. It is only *banah,* build.

A popular theory concerning the destination of the Hebrew epistle is that it was sent to Christians at Rome. Its closing, however, bears the greeting, "They of Italy salute you." This sounds as though it was written *from* Rome rather than *to* Rome, but it could refer to Italians living elsewere. The RSV excludes other interpretations by rendering the passage, "those who come from Italy send you greeting."

John A. Scott of Northwestern University wrote this of the RSV's rendition of Luke 1:3 in the *Classical Weekly* of January 6, 1947: "This version has, 'It seemed good to me also having followed closely for some time past . . . .' To translate the fine Greek word meaning 'from the beginning' with the tame 'for some time past' seems irony, not an intended transla-tion . . .".[7] Such minimizing of Luke's work in this translation fits the current source theories advocated by the liberals.

SAFEGUARDS

The RSV published two booklets explaining the work on the Old Testament and the New Testament. They were "written by members of the Committee and designed to help the general public to understand the main principles which have guided this comprehensive revision of the King James and American Standard versions."[8] In 1971 the second edition of the New Testament was published. The longer ending of Mark (16:9-20) and the pericope of the woman taken in adultery are restored to the text, accompanied by notes. The RSV has been published in several study editions: *Concordia Bible with Notes—New Testa-ment RSV,* the *New Oxford Annotated Bible, Harper's Study Bible,* the *RSV Common Bible,* and Zondervan's *The Layman's Parallel Bible.*

Good News Bible (Today's English Version)

TRANSLATOR(S)   Robert G. Bratcher, assisted by members of the Translations Department, American Bible Society and a Consultative Committee. Prepared under the auspices of the American Bible Society.

DATE   1976

PUBLISHER   American Bible Society and the United Bible Societies

TEXTUAL BASIS   Masoretic Text printed in *Biblia Hebraica* (3rd edition, 1937) edited by Rudolf Kittel; *The Greek New Testament*, United Bible Societies.

TYPE OF TRANSLATION   New translation of free style.

ACCURACY

Fair. Although the free translation will not show detailed accuracy, the message comprehension must be improved to justify its moving from the literal. Often this is not the case in the GNB. For example, *Before the world was created* (John 1:1) is used to paraphrase *In the beginning,* but it is unnecessary. Deep passages are like unopened packages. John chose to hand the reader an unopened package *(In the beginning),* but the translator interjects himself and says, "Here, let me open the package for you. What John means to say is 'the beginning of the world.' " This is not a service to the reader but simply deprives him of the joy of opening the package himself as he contemplates how the Word is prior to all beginnings. In like manner the translator mars the ultimate in simplicity and profundity, *and the Word was God,* by rendering it *and he was the same as God.* The translator has only succeeded in making fuzzy what is sharp in the Greek. While the passage is difficult to understand, it does not help to make it shallow by introducing a translation pointing to God-like instead of God. The word order and the absence of the article have their significance in the Greek, but they still point to an accurate English as simple and startling as the Greek, *and the Word was God.*

Bratcher is more successful than most in presenting a fresh, new, free translation and at the same time preserving the true thrust of the text. Frequently a person will react to a rendering and then check on it, only to find that the idea is right there in the original. But the instances of welcome enlightenment cannot always compensate for the shortcomings.

BEAUTY

Fair. The literary quality is judged differently by different people. The style is simple and direct, but one feels he is on a choppy sea rather than on a swift flowing stream. It is marred by such unnecessary expressions as "May you and your money go to hell . . ." (Acts 8:20).

The format of the GNB uses two columns to the page. This is a disadvantage in reading but makes the book a convenient size.

One of the distinguishing characteristics of the GNB is that the text is illustrated with line drawings by Mlle. Annie Vallotton. At first these caricatures seem out of place, but then interest in them grows. One wonders whether the style and application are a part of the authentic Bible message.

CLARITY

Good. The work was designed to meet the needs of non-Christian readers as well as Christians, those who have limited formal education, and those who have learned English as a second language. With these especially in mind, the translation comes through with clarity in an instructive way.

THEOLOGICAL BACKGROUND

Dr. Robert Bratcher is Southern Baptist.

WEAKNESSES

Unwise changes

The Greek word for *virgin* is rendered simply *girl* most of the time (eleven out of fourteen); for example, "He had a message for a girl . . ." (Luke 1:27). Although there may be little significance in some *virgin* passages, the references to Mary, the mother of Jesus, must be left clear in each instance. Changing the translation to *girl* is not a necessity of sacrificing detailed accuracy for the sake of a clearer message. It is not because *virgin* is obsolete, or that Bratcher wants to avoid using it. He even includes *virgin* when the Greek word for it is not used, but the meaning is clear: "Mary said to the angel, 'I am a virgin. How, then, can this be? ' (Luke 1:34), but omits it when Scripture states it as a fact (1:27). This instance becomes more puzzling when one realizes that between the 1966 edition of the GNB and the later editions Bratcher changed the translation from *virgin* to *girl* (1:27). The translator uses the word *virgin* in Matthew 1:23 when Isaiah's prophecy is quoted, but in the Old

Testament passage he uses *young woman* in the text instead of *virgin* (Isaiah 7:14).

The Greek word for *blood* is rendered *death;* for example, "For by the death of Christ we are set free . . ." (Ephesians 1:7). The issue is not whether at times *death* can be substituted for *blood* without loss of meaning, whether *death* is more contemporary or less repulsive than *blood,* nor whether Bratcher dislikes the word (he uses the term almost as many times as he omits it). This is a question of the wisdom of altering a figure used in the Scriptural account, especially in a matter as central as the atonement of Christ, so deep in meaning that man is not prepared to explain the full significance of the term, and at a point in which some liberal theology has associated it with antiquity and finds no place for it in "modern Christianity." It is a responsibility to retain the term both for contemporary need as well as faithfulness to the original.

One must commend Bratcher, however, for changing his rendition of Romans 1:17, "it is through faith alone from beginning to end . . . ." In later editions he has omitted "alone," which does not appear in the Greek. Another good change is at Matthew 5:17. In the NASB it reads, "I did not come to abolish, but to fulfill." In the early edition, the GNB read, "I have not come to do away with them, but to give them real meaning." This has since been changed to, "I have not come to do away with them, but to make their teachings come true." This is better, but to *fulfill* is better yet.

Misleading renderings

"On Saturday evening we gathered together for the fellowship meal . . ." (Acts 20:7, GNB). Compare this with a more literal translation: "And on the first day of the week, when we were gathered together to break bread . . ." (NASB). Both *Saturday evening* and *fellowship meal* are interpretation instead of translation in the GNB.

"Some of the supernatural beings saw that these girls were beautiful . . ." (Genesis 6:2). Compare this with another free translation, but closer to the original: "the sons of God, looking at the daughters of men, saw they were pleasing . . ." (*Jerusalem*

Bible). That these sons of God were supernatural beings is highly questionable and should not be written in the text of the translation.

"Make certain you do not perform your religious duties in public so that people will see what you do" (Matthew 6:1, GNB). Compare this with a better rendering: "Be careful not to make a show of your religion before men" *(New English Bible)*. Jesus is not declaring against religion in public but against making a show of religion to gain attention.

"I have complete confidence in the gospel" (Romans 1:16, GNB) says something different than "For I am not ashamed of the gospel" (NASB).

Nonpreferred renderings

The use of *respectable* in the place of *righteous* (Luke 5:32)

"But I know there is someone in heaven" (Job 19:25, GNB) for "I know that my Redeemer lives" (NASB)

"And your house will be my home as long as I live" for the last line of the twenty-third Psalm

SAFEGUARDS

The helps in the GNB are outstanding. Besides the usual notes, references to other passages dealing with similar matters are included at the bottom of the pages. A word list in the back serves as a dictionary for unfamiliar terms. Maps, chronological charts, and a subject index are also included in the back. Perhaps most helpful of all are introductions and outlines that precede each book of the GNB. Centered headings are included in the text to introduce each change in subject.

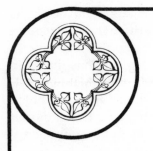

The Living Bible, Paraphrased

TRANSLATOR(S) Kenneth Taylor

DATE 1971

PUBLISHER Tyndale House, Wheaton, Illinois; Coverdale House, London, England

TYPE OF TRANSLATION Paraphrase:

To paraphrase is to say something in different words than the author used. It is a restatement of an author's thoughts, using different words than he did. . . . There are dangers in paraphrases, as well as values. For whenever the author's exact words are not translated from the original languages, there is a possibility that the translator, however honest, may be giving the English reader something that the original writer did not mean to say . . .[9]

ACCURACY

Poor. It would be unfair to require of a paraphrase the same formal-detail accuracy expected of a translation. On the other hand, the paraphrase must present such clarity and impact of the authentic message to justify departing from the wording and form of the original. In this area *The Living Bible* is deficient. Innovations appear without helping the message or the proper impact. The Psalms and Proverbs lack something when written in prose instead of the poetic form. A "P.S." tacked onto Paul's letter to the Philippians leaves a false impression. The prologue to Luke's Gospel in this paraphrase sounds as though Luke's work was simply rechecking previous accounts without going to the early disciples and eyewitnesses himself (compare with Luke 1:1-4, NASB). Whether a work is a translation or a paraphrase, it must be faithful to the meaning, intent, and impact of the original.

BEAUTY

Fair. If beauty meant readability, then *The Living Bible* would rank high. Literally millions have thrilled to its words. Some, however, comparing it with the beauty of the *King James Version* consciously or unconsciously, consider it inferior. But this is not a fair comparison. The English literary quality of the *King James Version* may be above the Greek literary quality of the New Testament; the best translation would be on the same level. But the English literary quality of the Living Bible seems below the literary level of New Testament Greek.

CLARITY

Good. If clarity were the only criterion, *The Living Bible* would be outstanding. "Its purpose is to say as exactly as possible what the writers of the Scripture meant, and to say it simply, expanding where necessary for a clear understanding by the modern reader."[10] This is the worthy goal held before Kenneth Taylor, the corps of Greek and Hebrew experts who checked for content, and the English critics who made suggestions for style. They have succeeded in presenting a clear, fast-moving narrative that has drawn the interest of many. It has been effective in evangelizing the nonbeliever. It has spoken to a generation of youth. But the worth of its clarity is diluted just to that degree to which it does not do what it set out to do—"to say as exactly as possible what the writers of the Scripture meant." All too often the idea in the paraphrased passage is not the idea of the Scripture.

THEOLOGICAL BACKGROUND
Evangelical.

WEAKNESSES
Crude or vulgar expressions
"Illegitimate bastard" (John 9:34)
"Whitewashed pigpen" (Acts 23:3)
"Barney the Preacher" (Acts 4:36)
Also 1 Kings 18:27

Influence of a personal theological slant
"I was born a sinner" (Psalm 51:5)
"We started out bad, being born with evil natures . . ." (Ephesians 2:3)
". . . favor with God by faith alone" (Romans 4:12)
"Great Tribulation" is written with the initial letters capitalized for the benefit of the premillennialist (Revelation 7:14)

Questionable interpretation written into the text
"Evil beings from the spirit world" (Genesis 6:4), instead of "sons of God"
"And everyone present was filled with the Holy Spirit" (Acts 2:4) excluding an alternate interpretation that it was only the apostles
"In baptism we show that we have been saved from death" (1 Peter 3:21) instead of the literal "baptism now saves you"
"Then he took a glass of wine" (Luke 22:17) for the literal "cup" or "fruit of the vine"

Freedom contributing to confusion

"[Premature] death" (Hebrews 5:7) does not add to the understanding of the passage.

"You are Peter, a stone; and upon this rock . . ." (Matthew 16:18) is an expansion for the commentary.

"Seven churches in Turkey" (Revelation 1:4, 11) is scarcely worth the anachronism in the text.

SAFEGUARDS

Frequent footnotes give literal renderings and/or alternate interpretations.

New International Version

TRANSLATOR(S)   Over one hundred participants divided into translation teams, Intermediate Committees (O.T. and N.T.), General Editorial Committee, and Translation Committee and literary consultants. Edwin H. Palmer, Executive Secretary.

DATE   1978

PUBLISHER   Sponsored by the New York International Bible Society; published by Zondervan.

TEXTUAL BASIS   Eclectic: Kittel's, Nestle's, and United Bible Society's texts.

TYPE OF TRANSLATION   New translation, free in style.

ACCURACY

Good. Although this is a free translation, it attempts to acknowledge each Hebrew or Greek word in some way—if not by a word in the English, then at least by word order, punctuation, or some device. It is contemporary in selection of words, and emulates the mood as well as the message of a passage. In some ways, it is closer to the Greek than most former translations; for example, in 2 Timothy 3:16, for "inspired of God" the NIV has "all Scripture is God-breathed."

BEAUTY

Good. The NIV combines a dignity suitable for use in public worship with a freshness of expression. This is not the beauty of the *King James Version*, but it has a contemporary beauty without being trite. Many editions are available, both single- and double-column; the format is pleasing and has frequent paragraphs. Verse designations are small and footnotes are kept to a minimum in order not to slow the progress of the reader.

CLARITY

Excellent. This version has been refined through a four-tiered committee approach, resulting in more checking and cross-checking than the known procedure of any other translation work. The product gives evidence of this scrutiny. The language is contemporary and the meaning is clear. But complete consistency is never accomplished. Some difficult or easily misunderstood words are rendered in a newer way: *Propitiation* (Romans 3:25) becomes *sacrifice of atonement* (is this any clearer?). In other places, however, difficult words are left in the text: *phylacteries* (Matthew 23:5) and *tetrarch* (Luke 9:7). Absolute consistency need not be demanded, but it may have been wiser to leave the former unchanged in the text and explained by a footnote, and the latter changed in the text.

THEOLOGICAL BACKGROUND

Evangelical. The translators "are all committed to the full authority and complete trustworthiness of the Scriptures which they believe to be God's Word in written form."[11]

WEAKNESSES
At times free to an extreme

The word for *flesh* in the Greek is *sarx*. In the NIV the word *sarx* is translated *flesh* only thirty times out of 138 Greek uses. The next most frequent translation of the word is *sinful nature* (twenty-five times). But this rendering is more of an interpretation than a translation. Most of the other translations reviewed to this point render these passages simply *flesh*, except for one instance in the RSV. All but four of the *sinful nature* passages are confined to Galatians and Romans. When regarding the Son, however, *sarx* is translated *human nature* (Romans 1:3). The safest thing to do is leave the word with its primary meaning *(flesh)* and relegate the discussion to the commentary rather than write *sinful nature* into the text. This is carrying free translation too far.

Likewise in Luke 8:12 the translator has no right to write in, "so that they cannot believe." This is more than the Greek allows. The King James renders it, "lest they should believe and be saved."

Concern for the contemporary

Not only must a translator be sensitive to contemporary vocabulary, but also to contemporary issues. At the present, spiritual gifts are drawing much attention and are associated with the New Testament miraculous gifts of the Spirit, such as speaking in tongues and prophecy. It is inadvisable to write in *spiritual*, especially under these circumstances, when the word is not in the Greek (1 Peter 4:10). The word *spiritual* does not appear in 1 Corinthians 12, and by context this meaning may be justified in 12:4, but the context may be too far removed to justify writing *spiritual* in again in 1 Corinthians 1:7. The word for *spiritual* does appear with *gift* in Romans 1:11 and is rendered the expected way, *spiritual gift*.

Often the addition of an *and*, or its omission, is simply a matter of literary taste. But in the case of Revelation 20:4, an *and* has been omitted, a new sentence begun, and in this way "the souls of those who had been beheaded" are identified with those "who had not worshiped the beast or his image." Possibly the latter, however, may be an additional group, according to the Greek. This might be vital to one's interpretation of the millennium, the first resurrection, and Christ's reign. Regardless of what position one holds, it is important to allow in the English the interpretations that are allowed in the Greek.

It is also possible to allow contemporary concerns to take precedence over the actual Greek text. For example, Acts 7:36 and Hebrews 11:29 make reference to the Red Sea. The NIV carries a footnote at these places adding, "that is, the Sea of Reeds." There is no dispute about the Greek words meaning *Red Sea*. There is no crucial manuscript difference. The terminology of *Red Sea* is introduced from the Hebrew *yam sup* found in the Old Testament. This in turn introduces the question of the location of the Israelites' crossing, which in turn raises the question of the type of miracle involved, if any miracle at all. It is unnecessary to introduce this matter in a footnote, especially where the NIV's notes are kept to a minimum. A cross-reference to the Old Testament passage would be more appropriate than a note that implies that the Greek can be translated *Sea of Reeds*. Whether the terminology Red Sea includes the northern papyrus-marshes or whether the *yam-sup* includes the Gulf of Aqaba (see 1 Kings 9:26) is a matter for the commentary.

SAFEGUARDS

The notes are few but helpful. Each chapter is divided by subheadings showing the major subjects in the course of thought. These are especially good. One edition is printed with study helps, including subject index, a harmony of passages on the ministry of Jesus, notes on "How to Study the Bible," and maps. The preface gives a good rationale for a freer-type translation but "in the translation itself, brackets are occasionally used to indicate words or phrases supplied for clarification." The trustworthiness and readability of this translation commend its use in the coming years. Considerable revision was made between the publication of the New Testament (1973) and the whole Bible (1978). Constant revision is planned for the coming years. A thorough Study Edition of the NIV is in preparation; the publication date is projected for 1985.

Jerusalem Bible

TRANSLATOR(S)   Alexander Jones, general editor. Roman Catholic group of Biblical and literary experts, Joseph Leo Alston, J.R.R. Tolkien, and others.

DATE   1966

PUBLISHER   Doubleday & Company, Inc.

TEXTUAL BASIS   Eclectic: Masoretic and LXX of the Old Testament and a Greek text of the New, but simultaneously compared with the French *La Bible de Jerusalem.* "Over half of the textual notes in the JB New Testament (342/618) serve to indicate a Vulgate reading that has been displaced."[12]

TYPE OF TRANSLATION   "Although based on the French *Bible de Jerusalem,* the English version is not simply a translation from the French."[13]

115

A new, free translation. The translator of the Bible into a vernacular may surely consider himself free to remove the purely linguistic archaisms of that vernacular, but here his freedom ends. He may not, for example, substitute his own modern images for the old ones: the theologian and the preacher may be encouraged to do this but not the translator (Editor's Foreword, JB, p. vi).

ACCURACY

Fair. Although the elements of Catholicism and liberalism are present, they are restrained to attempt to present a translation acceptable to all. Textual readings may follow quotations from the early fathers too often, and the freedom of translation leads away from the text at times.[14]

BEAUTY

Fair. The JB is surprisingly fresh in spite of its simultaneous consideration of the French *La Bible de Jerusalem* and the Latin of Jerome, besides translating from the Hebrew, Aramaic, and Greek. But the results are somewhat uneven. Some expressions are outstanding, others awkward. Contemporary slang expressions are avoided.

CLARITY

Good. This is a readable and lively translation. The language is clear for the most part. Some rarer words creep in, however; for example, in Mark 12: "to be greeted obsequiously" (v. 38), "any holocaust or sacrifice" (v. 33).

THEOLOGICAL BACKGROUND

Roman Catholic, mixed with liberalism.

WEAKNESSES

Too free

In 1 Timothy 3:1, the JB has *presiding elder* to translate the Greek word for *bishop*. In a footnote on the passage the editors

116

explain: "The word *episcopos* used here by Paul had not yet acquired the same meaning as 'bishop.' This is an admission that the present Roman Catholic usage of the word *bishop* is not the way Paul uses the word in the Scriptures.

The doctrine of original sin is supported in rendering Psalm 51:5: "You know I was born guilty, a sinner from the moment of conception." Nothing is said of guilt in the Hebrew of this verse, and one is not justified in writing it into the translation.

The phrase used in the Scripture, *fruit of the vine,* is translated *wine:* "I tell you solemnly, I shall not drink any more wine until the day I drink the new wine in the kingdom of God" (Mark 14:25). Not only does this violate the translator's principle of retaining the figure used in the original, but nowhere in the Scripture is the Greek word for *wine* used for the cup of the Lord's Supper.

In the JB Galatians 5:12 is translated: "Tell those who are disturbing you I would like to see the knife slip." Regardless of what Paul is saying in this verse, it is inadmissible to render it that way. It is too free.

Correlation of translation and notes

The greatest strengths, and at the same time the greatest weaknesses, of the JB are in the introduction and notes. They are extensive and add much information. At times, however, they cloud the meaning of the translation text.

In the text of Matthew 13:55, 56, relatives of Jesus are clearly named as brothers and sisters: "And his brothers James and Joseph and Simon and Jude? His sisters, too, are they not all here with us?" But to protect the doctrine of the perpetual virginity of Mary, Matthew 12:46 has already been given a footnote: "Not Mary's children but near relations, cousins perhaps, which both Hebrew and Aramaic style 'brothers.' " At Matthew 1:25 a note states:

The text is not concerned with the period that followed and, taken by itself, does not assert Mary's perpetual virginity which, however, the gospels elsewhere suppose and which the Tradition of the church affirms.

117

In a similar way the primacy of Peter is treated under a note on Matthew 16:19:

> Catholic exegetes maintain that these enduring promises hold good not only for Peter himself but also for Peter's successors. This inference, not explicitly drawn in the text, is considered legitimate because Jesus plainly intends to provide for his church's future by establishing a regime that will not collapse with Peter's death.

On the whole, however, when not mixed with liberal theories, the notes are objective and helpful; for example, on Romans 6:4 the note affirms,

> Baptism is not separated from faith but goes with it. . . . The sinner is immersed in water (the etymological meaning of 'baptise' is 'dip') and thus 'buried' with Christ, Colossians 2:12, with whom also he emerges to resurrection, Romans 8:11f., as a 'new creature,' 2 Corinthians 5:17f., a 'new man,' Ephesians 2:15f., a member of the one Body animated by the one Spirit, 1 Corinthians 12:13, Ephesians 4:4f.

The introductions contain a mixture of liberalism and conservatism. Moses did not write the first five Biblical books bearing his name, according to the JB's introduction to the Pentateuch (JB, pp. 7, 8):

> Now modern Pentateuchal study has revealed a variety of style, lack of sequence, and repetitions in narrative which make it impossible to ascribe the whole work to a single author.
> So far as the book of Genesis is concerned it is not difficult to recognize and follow the threads of three traditions: Yahwistic, Elohistic, Priestly.

The translators proceed to use the form *Yahweh* to translate the tetragrammaton rendered "LORD" in the KJV and most English translations. It seems strange indeed to close the twenty-third Psalm with, "Ah how goodness and kindness pursue me, every day of my life; my home, the house of Yahweh, as long as I live." The use of the term *Yahweh* need not be associated with theories of denial that Moses wrote the Pentateuch, but this is the case in the introduction and notes of the JB. It puts them at variance with Jesus, who quoted from the Pentateuch as the words of Moses.

Common liberal theories are set down in the introduction. The unity of Isaiah is not allowed—"It is therefore probable that chapters 40-55 are the work of an unnamed writer at the end of the exilic period . . ." (p. 1125). The prophet Daniel lived to about 530 B.C., but his book is not attributed to him in the JB introduction—"The book must therefore have been written during the persecution under Antiochus Epiphanes and before his death . . . that is to say between 167 and 164" (p. 1132). According to the JB, 2 Peter is not written by the apostle Peter, although this is what 2 Peter claims—"This is what we should call forgery but what in those days literary convention found admissible" (p. 395). One should take issue with each of these conclusions as well as the grounds presented for them.

On the other hand, in Synoptic studies the JB denies the priority of Mark, and the existence of Q (initial of the German word *Quelle,* source) is declared an inadequate explanation of the similarities and differences among the Gospel writings. Rather, the JB emphasizes the apostolic origin and historic value of the Synoptics.

Paul is almost allowed to write the Pastoral Letters (1 Timothy, Titus, 2 Timothy) according to the introduction (p. 264), and Hebrews is considered to bear a relationship close enough to Paul to warrant its inclusion from early times in the *Corpus Paulinum* (p. 265).

The apocryphal books are arranged according to the order found in the LXX and Vulgate, except that 1 and 2 Maccabees are put with the Old Testament historical books. The Old Testament books are given under titles more familiar to Protestants than 1, 2, 3, and 4 Kings and 1 and 2 Paralipomenon of the Douay-Rheims. Also, in both Testaments Isaiah, Jeremiah, Hosea, etc. retain the same form instead of changing to Isaias, Jeremias, Osee, etc.

Strictly Catholic renderings, for example, *priests* for elders (Titus 1:5), or *do penance* for *repent* (Acts 2:38), which appear in the Douay-Rheims version, are not found in the JB.

SAFEGUARDS

The notes and introduction in the regular *Jerusalem Bible* edition (The Reader's Edition includes only the briefest of notes) are extensive and informative. They carry summary explanations of the latest in Biblical studies all the way from the texts and archeology to literary and exegetical works. It is almost a translation and commentary combined.

New King James Version

TRANSLATOR(S)

Translators, editors, and Overview Committee members for this work totaled 130 individuals. General editorship: O.T., first William White, then James Price; N.T., Arthur Farstad.

DATE

1982.

PUBLISHER

Thomas Nelson Publishers, Sam Moore, President.

TEXTUAL BASIS

(O.T.) *Biblia Hebraica* (Stuttgart, 1967-77) compared with Bomberg edition of 1524-25. (N.T.) the text used for the 1611 *King James Version* (referred to as *Textus Receptus* after 1633) and annotated with the similar readings of the Majority Text.

TYPE OF TRANSLATION

An updating of the *King James Version*. It remains close to its original in the revision, therefore literal in rendering the Greek and consistent in preserving the wording of the King James where it is considered accurate, clear, and contemporary.

ACCURACY

Good. Endangering its accuracy is the textual basis for the work. In the body of the translation it follows the *Textus Receptus* of the 1611 King James even if the Majority Text (see description, p. 67) and the Nestle/United Bible Societies Text both depart from it. For examples of this see 1 John 5:7, 8 and Luke 17:36. This means that no possibility is allowed for a single change based upon the findings in the thousands of manuscripts that have come to light since the seventeenth-century King James translation was made.

In spite of this negative feature, the accuracy is considered good in general:

1) Even though a great number of differences do exist between the manuscripts grouped as the Majority Text and those grouped as the Nestle/United Bible Societies' Text, there are relatively few examples of crucial changes involved in the decisions.

2) These points of differences are noted in the footnotes of the NKJV.

3) The NKJV keeps close to the Greek text and faithful to the context of meaning in its translation methods. Examples of changes for greater accuracy: dropping the word "unknown" from the description of the tongues referred to in 1 Corinthians 14:2ff; rendering "Passover" instead of "Easter" in Acts 12:4.

BEAUTY

Good. It is difficult to estimate how the beauty of this translation will be judged after a passage of time. It seems to have retained much of the cadence and majesty of the 1611 King James, but it may have lost some of its older charm through the very deleting of the archaisms. Furthermore, the fact that it is a literal translation of necessity hinders the natural flow of expression in the English. Nevertheless this revision is not crude and patchy. It introduces a dignity and forceful grandeur of its own. For example, read 1 Corinthians 13:1ff. It sounds familiar, but note some changes that are improvements but do not mar the beauty: instead of "tinkling cymbal" (not characteristic of cymbals), the NKJV has "clanging cymbal;" instead of "charity vaunteth not itself," the wording is changed to "love does not parade itself."

CLARITY
Good. Few would deny that for today's reader, the NKJV is a great improvement in clarity over the 1611 original translation. The work could have gone considerably further in making changes to clarify and especially to give a smooth, contemporary English, but this would have resulted in losing more of its identity with the early *King James Version*. The results as they are remain good, a combination of the old and the new, but they reflect a desire to preserve rather than change, even though further clarification was possible.

From many examples of good changes, note the use of "Holy Spirit" instead of "Holy Ghost" at all times; see also such passages as 2 Corinthians 10:16b, "and not to boast in another man's line of things made ready to our hand," which has been made understandable in the NKJV, "and not to boast in another man's sphere of accomplishment."

More changes have been made than most realize. In the first chapter of Luke alone, well over three hundred alterations have been made in wording, punctuation, and format.

THEOLOGICAL BACKGROUND
Evangelical. Each who worked on the project accepted the Scriptures as the uniquely inspired Word of God.

WEAKNESSES
Precedence among criteria
The choice to follow the Greek text of the *King James Version* (1611) gives unwarranted precedence to the *Textus Receptus* (see above). Although much careful work has gone into the publishing of the Majority Text, the real use of this study has been

thwarted by following whatever the King James reads whether supported by the Majority Text or not (for example, over 15 instances in the Gospel of Luke). Whether one agrees with advocates of the Majority Text in their consistent preference for its readings, one must recognize the healthy corrective that has been imposed on the Westcott-Hort tradition and long accepted assumptions in this area of textual criticism. It still stands, however, that as long as the body of the NKJV follows the Greek text of the 1611 version in every instance, it is accepting this as an absolute in its criteria. This should not be.

A second criterion is directly related to the first, and raises further question. Does the King James translation of 1611 occupy as absolute a role in translation work as has been given the *Textus Receptus* in the Greek text? This revision of the King James has been undertaken in part to honor the King James translation and assure its continuing use. But will this criterion of preserving the King James be given precedence over clearly communicating truth in a contemporary language? Something deeper is involved than honoring the *King James Version*. If, for example, one wishes to honor Shakespeare and seeks to assure continued study of his work, one does not do so by updating his wording and changing his punctuation. One must acknowledge that something more is involved in revising the King James, or else no revision would have been undertaken. The foremost motive is not to honor the *King James Version* but to communicate the Word of God in the best possible way. At times, however (not all the time by any means), it seems that in the NKJV the 1611 King James was given a position above a translation to be revised and made a model to be preserved.

The following are two examples of places where changes should have been made: Luke was not writing his Gospel to provide an account of what was believed in the early church (so the NKJV at Luke 1:1), but what was actually fulfilled, or was accomplished, or happened (this is the first meaning of the word and it is rendered as such in a score of current translations). In Luke 18:12 the Pharisee does not claim to tithe all he possesses, but rather all he acquires (his income, not his capital).

124

Private interpretation

Some changes that do appear in the NKJV cannot be explained by a difference in the Greek text, or by what was in the 1611 version, or by the demands of contemporary usage. Only the favoring of a particular interpretation has been served. Giving but one example, a passage reflects the dispensational view—when"it is near" is changed in the NKJV to "He is near" (Matthew 24:33).

SAFEGUARDS

Footnotes

Ironically, the dispute over the Greek text used for the translation work has resulted in one of the greatest assets of this revision. To safeguard the work concerning the text, footnotes have been included to give information concerning those points where the Majority Text and the Nestle/United Bible Societies Text differ. Also since the *Textus Receptus* holds its place at all times in the body of the revision, one is able to compare its reading with the other two as well. This is very helpful. No other current English translation has as much information in this area.

Helps

Words are italicized that have been added in the English but do not have a direct counterpart in the Greek. This practice was used in the 1611 work as well. Old Testament quotations are given in a different type face, and citations are included in the footnotes.

CONCLUDING NOTE

an one English translation of the Bible be recommended above all others? This final question cannot be answered by a simple "yes" or "no." It depends on what a person wants most in the Bible he reads.

If he desires beautiful language, coupled with a respect for the past, with a ring of authenticity and familiarity, the *King James Version* will be the selection. Its language is associated with the past, but this is not entirely against the King James. After all, Jesus lived in a certain time and place in the past. If one makes Jesus so contemporary that he cuts all ties to the past, this leaves Him as unhistorical. God did become flesh and lived among us in the person of His Son. The *King James Version* conveys this fact to the heart of the reader or hearer. If one gets the feeling that this book has a quality different from other books, this, too, is in line with the truth. Although it is not the literary quality that makes the difference, the dignity and depth of the *King James Version* is commensurate with the importance of God's communication with man. The *New King James Version* retains much of the good qualities of the earlier version, and is recommended for today's generation in the place of the 1611 King James.

If one is approaching the Bible to study its words and concepts in a careful, comparative way, the *New American Standard Bible* is the best selection. This translation is accurate in form and detail. Using this translation with its helps, and with a Bible concordance and a Bible dictionary, one can dig to new depths of understanding. Wherever he puts his shovel into its soil, he will unearth new treasures. But a translation cannot be both literal and natural at the same time. Although the NASB can be read with pleasure and understanding, the translation tends to become heavy with conscious adherence to the idioms of Hebrew or Greek.

The reader has still further needs. It is good to read a translation for the pure desire of receiving a fresh, clear message from God. There is the danger that one may archaize Jesus and leave Him bound to the first century. He really lived then, but He really lives now, too. The contemporary, readable language of the *New International Version* fills the need of making the Bible come alive for today's reader. With its high measure of accuracy and beauty this translation contributes to the joy of reading God's Word in hours of meditation and discussion. Whether in the church or the home, whether for the Christian or the non-Christian, this version speaks in a vivid way.

The *King James Version* retains the beauty and majesty of the English language at its best and the *New King James* adds more clarity and readibility to its forebear. The *New American Standard Bible* presents an accurate, literal translation of Scripture, admirable for study in God's Word. The *New International Version* breathes with the freshness of God's living Word in a free-flowing expression—true and clear. Whether this combination or another, one needs to select with care translations of the Scripture, God's Word for people in every generation. Faithfulness is the keynote of translating God's Word—both in word and deed.

POINTS TO PONDER

1. What do you expect of a good translation of the Bible?

2. What helps are most beneficial in a Bible?
3. Which translations do you prefer? Why?

1See O. T. Allis, *The New English Bible: A Comparative Study* (1963).
2See F. F. Bruce, *The English Bible: A History of Translation* (1970), pp. 248ff.
3See O. T. Allis, *Revision or New Translation? The Revised Standard Version of 1946* (1948).
4See Burton L. Goddard, "Goddard on RSV," *United Evangelical Action,* March 1, 1953.
5F. F. Bruce, p. 194.
6See R. C. Foster, *The Revised Standard Version of the New Testament: An Appraisal,* and *The Revised Standard Version: A Reply to Dr. Clarence T. Craig.*
7Cited in R. C. Foster, *The Battle of the Versions* (1953), p. 8.
8Preface to the *Revised Standard Version,* p. xiv.
9From the preface to *The Living Bible.*
10From the preface to *The Living Bible*
11Preface to the *New International Version,* p. viii.
12Errol F. Rhodes, "Text of NT in Jerusalem and New English Bible," *Catholic Biblical Quarterly,* 32 (1970), p. 49.
13John J. Delaney, editor, Doubleday & Co., quoted in *What Bible Can You Trust?* Broadman Press (1974), p. 61.
14See Gordon D. Fee, "The Text of John in the Jerusalem Bible," *Journal of Biblical Literature,* 90 (1970), pp. 167-173.